The Business Bible

The Business Bible

10 New Commandments for
Bringing Spirituality & Ethical
Values into the Workplace

Rabbi Wayne Dosick

For People of All Faiths, All Backgrounds
JEWISH LIGHTS Publishing
Woodstock, Vermont

The Business Bible: 10 New Commandments for Bringing Spirituality & Ethical Values into the Workplace

Library of Congress Cataloging-in-Publication Data

Dosick, Wayne D., 1947–
The business bible : 10 new commandments for bringing spirituality & ethical values into the workplace / Wayne Dosick.
    p. cm.
Rev. ed. of: The business bible : ten new commandments for creating an ethical workplace. New York : HarperBusiness, 1994.
Includes bibliographical references.
ISBN 1-58023-101-2 (pbk.)
1. Business ethics. 2. Ethics in the Bible. 3. Business—Religious aspects—Judaism. I. Title: Ten new commandments for bringing spirituality and ethical values into the workplace. II. Title.

HF5387 .D67 2000
174'.4—dc21
                                                     00-055857

10 9 8 7 6 5 4 3 2 1

Manufactured in the United States of America

Cover design by Bridgett Taylor

For People of All Faiths, All Backgrounds
Published by Jewish Lights Publishing
A Division of LongHill Partners, Inc.
Sunset Farm Offices, Route 4, P.O. Box 237
Woodstock, VT 05091
Tel: (802) 457-4000   Fax: (802) 457-4004
www.jewishlights.com

Contents

~

CONTENTS

as the soda-pop bottle teaches

No Deposit

No Return

In the Beginning

~

My telephone rang at eleven-thirty at night.

In a quivering voice the caller said, "Hello, Rabbi. I'm sorry to bother you so late, but I have to see you. It can't wait until morning. Can I come to your house right now?"

In no more than fifteen minutes, a man I had known for more than a decade was at my front door.

"I'm in big trouble, Rabbi," he said. "No, I'm all right. My wife, the kids, they're fine. But, I just don't know what to do.

"You know my company. Almost all the work we do is for the government. My job is to write the reports, to certify that we have done all the work exactly to the specifications we have been given. Tomorrow I have to turn in the final report for the project we've been working on for the last year and a half.

"Rabbi, I've gone over the numbers again and again, a hundred times, maybe two hundred times, and they come up the same every time. The parts we've built just don't match the standards we were given. They're deficient. And that's what I wrote in the first draft of my report.

"But at five o'clock today, my boss came to me and said, 'Listen, we can't turn in this report. If we do, we'll lose millions of dollars in payments and penalties, and we probably won't get another government contract for years. You've got to fix up the numbers and make the report come out okay. Now, rewrite this report and have it on my desk by nine o'clock tomorrow morning.'

"I was stunned. I didn't know what to say. I figured that my report might cause some trouble, but here my boss is telling me to change it, to make up numbers, to write a report that I know isn't true.

"I said, 'I can't do that. I know that there'll be problems, but you can't expect me to make up numbers and lie to the government.'

"And do you know what he did, Rabbi? He stared right at me for fifteen, twenty seconds, and then he said, 'Have the new report on my desk by nine o'clock tomorrow morning.'

"He didn't threaten me or anything, but I got the message: 'Do what I say, or your career here is as good as finished. Maybe I can't fire you, but I sure can make it miserable here for you. You'll wind up in some dead-end little job, or maybe supervising our branch office in Siberia.'

"What am I going to do, Rabbi? I can't make up numbers out of thin air. I can't lie on a report to the government. But I've got a wife, kids, a mortgage to pay, a career to think about. What am I going to do?"

Rabbis—like priests, ministers, and imams—are often viewed as "holy" people—somewhat different, and even isolated, from the people and events around us.

We are usually asked questions about belief and faith, piety and prayer, spirit and sanctity.

Yet here at midnight was a deeply troubled man, turning to me for counsel over a dilemma from his workaday business world.

He came to me because he knew that I would not speak for myself alone, but from out of the depths of the religious sources and traditions that I teach.

And he knew that religious teachings are not "other-worldly" or distant, but are immediate and compelling, so extraordinarily relevant and so very useful, offering guidance and direction for every aspect of life—if only he would choose to use them.

A soapmaker once came to a rabbi. He said, "Rabbi, Rabbi, what good is religion? Religion teaches honesty. But just look at how many dishonest people there are. And religion promises peace in the world. But just look at how many wars there have been. What good is religion?"

The rabbi answered, "My dear soapmaker, there are so many wonderful soaps in the world. And yet just look at how many dirty people there are."

Religion—like soap—works when you use it.

The religious quest deals not simply with the world of the spirit, but with the world of the ordinary and the practical—because that is where you live.

The Bible and later sacred literature guide you and teach you the way to live and act and make choices—not just in a synagogue, church, or mosque—but everywhere, every moment of every day.

These holy books are filled with precepts and principles governing the "nitty-gritty" of your workaday world—in the street and in the marketplace, in trade and in commerce.

The Bible is filled with *civil legislation* requiring, among other things, that business be conducted with honor and integrity; that people treat each other with kindness and dignity; that workers be protected; that health and welfare be safeguarded; that profits be shared with those who help earn them.

The Bible deals with the most earthy of matters: how to earn a living while living decently, how to be productive and prosperous while being honest, just, and fair.

The wisdom of religious teaching lies right in the arena of the factory and the shop, the store and the road, the office and the boardroom—guiding you, teaching you, inspiring you, to do your best and to be your best.

In the American business community, there is a growing awareness that ancient wisdom has much to inform and influence the modern marketplace.

After decades of unparalleled growth and prosperity, in the aftermath of financial scandal, and in the midst of difficult financial times, the business world has been moved to an almost unprecedented soul-searching and self-examination.

Prominent—and highly successful—business leaders who, not too long ago, described the workplace only as a place for production and profit are now speaking about a business world defined by *"mission, vision, and values,"* a place where there are not only contracts but a *"covenant,"* a place where workers can find *"real meaning"* in their work, and where good management is a matter of *"love…a calling…a trust."*

This newly evolving business design—rooted, as it is, in age-old religious traditions—led *Fortune* magazine to proclaim that *"the language of the pulpit* has become the currency of the executive suite."

By bringing the ancient truths and enduring values of the religious and spiritual quest into the modern marketplace, the contemporary business world can be transformed into a place where accomplishment and satisfaction, honesty and integrity, mutual commitment and personal growth, decency and dignity are the everyday guides and goal.

In this *Business Bible*, you will learn how to create—for yourself and for those with whom you work—an ethical—and a meaningful—workplace. You will learn how to do *well* and, at the very same time, how to do *good*.

~

You will come to understand:

- Why *vision* is more than what you see;
- Why *value* means more than net worth;
- How *building community* builds business;
- Why the *worth ethic* is as important as the work ethic;
- How *developing people* can develop business;
- How *business ethics* lead to business excellence.

Ten Commandments were enough for Moses to bring down from the mountain, for he lived in much simpler times.

Our world is much more complex, much more complicated, much more challenging than his.

For us, the original ten—as important and as enduring as they are—are not enough.

We need more.

We need commandments to guide us in the workaday world of our jobs, our businesses, our professions.

So, here—steeped in antiquity and clothed in contemporary garb—are Ten Commandments for Creating an Ethical Workplace—the ways to bring meaning and worth, values and ethics, into the modern marketplace.

Come on the journey.

Join in the quest.

The promised land of professional achievement and personal fulfillment awaits you.

The First Commandment

~

"YOUR EAR

SHALL HEAR;

YOUR EYES

SHALL SEE"

A few weeks ago, a colleague and I were walking down a crowded, noisy city street when she said to me, "Listen to the chirping of the birds. Don't they make a beautiful sound?"

I was amazed by what she was saying. "Are you joking?" I asked. "There's too much noise—all the cars and trucks, the blaring horns, the ambulance sirens, people shouting at each other above the din. It's impossible to hear the sound of a tiny bird in all this racket."

We walked a little farther.

My friend opened her purse, took out a quarter, and tossed it on the ground. The coin bounced on the sidewalk, plinking as it rolled.

Half a dozen people—stopped by the sound of the quarter

hitting the pavement—followed its rolling path and stooped to pick it up.

We hear what we want to hear.

The art of doing business depends on how well you hear, how well you listen.

How many stories have you heard about the silly—and the tragic—mistakes that have been made, the expectations that have been dashed, the deals that have been lost, the reputations that have been ruined, when someone doesn't listen well.

The shipping clerk sends a package to London, England, instead of London, Ontario, because he didn't listen.

The secretary sends the contract to Mr. Brown in Clarksville instead of to Mr. Clark in Brownsville because she didn't listen.

The stockbroker sends the entire market into chaos when he sells fifty million shares instead of fifty million dollars' worth of shares because he didn't listen.

Should you meet your customer in Rio or Reno? It all depends on how well you listen.

Is the order for ten or for a ton? It all depends on how well you listen.

Is the meeting here or there? Is the call trivial or urgent? Is the offer flimsy or firm? Is the time to act now or later? It all depends on how well you listen.

How well you listen depends on two people—the listener *and* the speaker.

The first half of listening well is being spoken to—or speaking—clearly.

When you want people to listen *to you,* you can begin by making sure that your words are simple, direct, and distinct.

How many times have the "idea folks" complained that the production team just can't turn their ideas into reality? And how many times has the manufacturing side complained that the "concepts people" really have no idea what it takes to make a product?

How many times have both the "creative people" and the "money people" thrown up their hands in frustration, complaining, "How often do we have to say the same thing? They just don't get it. *We're not even talking the same language.*"

Professor of Linguistics Deborah Tannen, in her book *You Just Don't Understand,* contends that "men and women live in different worlds, even under the same roof—so conversation between them is like cross-cultural communication."

If men and women—husbands and wives in the most intimate of relationships—have trouble communicating, and understanding each other at home, it is very likely that coworkers may have the same kind of difficulty—or worse—at the office.

And—regardless of gender—people with different backgrounds, different education, different training, and different agendas may simply not hear and understand what is being said.

It is very possible that people trained in scientific research *really don't* have the vocabulary and the language to understand the intricacies of technical production. And it is very possible that people trained to be creative thinkers *really don't* have the vocabulary and the language to understand the precise details of accounting and finance.

All too often, people are really *not* speaking "the same language."

A number of years ago, I attended a professional football game. Much to my (obviously naive) amazement, two young men in the seats a few rows ahead of me spent most of the game cutting and snorting lines of cocaine.

Later that night—still rather astounded—I spoke to a friend on the phone: "You really won't believe what I saw at the game today," I said. "Two guys, sitting right in front of me, spent the whole game snorting coke."

A few days later, I heard my then five-year-old son reporting to his little friend what he had overheard me say on the telephone. "You won't believe what my dad saw at the football game," he said. "There were two guys in the row ahead of him who were so rude that all through the game, they *slurped their Cokes.*"

He heard what he was capable of hearing.

To make sure that *you* are heard, you can try to speak the language of the person you are addressing.

To make sure that you are understood, you can try to be sensitive to your listener's experience and perceptions, and speak words that your listener can comprehend.

The other half of listening is taking the time and the energy to listen to what is really being said, to hear the words—spoken and, sometimes, unspoken—that are being uttered.

What does your boss *really* mean when she says, "I need you to stay late tonight to finish up this project"?

Does she mean, "It doesn't matter to me that you have to pick up your child from day care and that you might have plans for tonight"?

Or does she mean, "I'm really worried that this project won't be done on time, and the entire department's reputation—and maybe my job—is at stake on this one. And I really don't think that I can do it alone. So will you please stay and help me?"

What does your employee *really* mean when she says, "I must have this Tuesday off, no matter what"?

Does she mean, "I don't care about doing my share of the workload here"?

Or does she mean, "My elderly father is ill and he has to go to the doctor on Tuesday, and if I don't take him, he has no way to get there. And besides, I'm pretty worried about my dad."

What does your customer *really* mean when he says, "I'm sorry, I just can't order anything from you this month"?

Does he mean, "I got a better deal from your competitor"?

Or does he mean, "Business is really tough and I just don't have the cash to buy any more inventory, but I'm really too proud to tell you"?

When you listen well, you might be able to hear the hidden agenda, the unexpressed needs—the fears and the ambivalence, or the confidence and the certainty.

When you listen well—and really, really hear—you can come a long way toward understanding and, ultimately, succeeding.

You can find the balance between speaking and listening by learning when to speak up and when to keep quiet.

Sometimes you are so eager to give your own ideas, to offer your own advice, to make your own proposals—or just to hear yourself talk—that you open your mouth but close your ears.

You don't listen to what others have to say.

You don't hear someone else's good idea.

You ignore someone else's plan—no matter how good it might be.

You pay no heed to someone else's passion—no matter how motivating it might become.

You forget how much there is to hear, and how much there is to learn.

So the old camp rule is as good in the boardroom, the office, and the store, with coworkers, colleagues, and customers, as it was in the cabins at camp: Sometimes you accomplish the most with "mouths closed; ears open."

There is one more art of listening that you can acquire.

You can listen not only to the words but to the sound of the voice.

How many times has this happened to you? You pick up the phone and say, "Hello."

From the other end of the line, your mother says, "So what's wrong?"

"There's nothing wrong, Mom."

"Don't tell me. I can hear. There's *something* wrong."

If your mom can do it, then—with less success, but with frequent accuracy—so can you.

People can use words to try to fake or fool, but eventually the tone and the timbre of their voice lay open the truth.

In your voice—and the voices of the people to whom you listen—is your exhaustion or your exhilaration, your anger or your joy, your deception or your honesty.

When you listen carefully, the sounds of the voice you hear will reveal what you need to know.

A dapper, sophisticated college student once asked how he might become a scintillating conversationalist.

The wise old professor who was asked the question responded, "Listen, my son…."

"Yes, yes," the student said. "Go on."

"That is all," replied the professor. "Just listen."

When the telephone rings and rings, when your colleagues, coworkers and customers talk and talk and talk, when the noises of the world threaten to engulf you, instead of "tuning out"—as it would be so tempting to do—you can try to "tune in."

You can listen—really, really listen—to what is being said to you.

And you can listen, too, for the sounds of silence.

When you listen to the song of the heart that is being opened to you, you can open *your* heart to hear.

But even listening well is not enough.
It is not your ears alone that need to be open.
Your eyes need to see.

One day the president of a large firm was walking through the halls of his company's building, checking into office after office, work station after work station.

One of his assistants followed him, clipboard in hand, making notes of all the president's impressions, the orders he issued, the changes he wanted to make.

The president came to a large corner office where the occupant was sitting, feet up on her desk, just staring out the window.

The president said to his assistant, "Just look at that woman. She is doing nothing but staring out her window. She is not getting any work done. She is wasting time and money. Fire her immediately."

"But sir," the assistant said, "that woman is our vice president in charge of ideas. Some of the best projects that this company has done in recent years were her ideas. We pay her to think, and she thinks best when she is sitting with her feet up on her desk, staring out the window."

"Well," huffed the president, caught in his own mistake, "well, then get her a *bigger* window."

Vision is more than what you see.
Vision is opening your eyes—and your mind's eye, as well—to that inner place where you see and foresee, where you dream and imagine and create.

The success of your company, your business, your profession, your career, depends on your vision.

You could be satisfied with the status quo. You could be content to leave things as they are. You could choose not to "rock the boat," "upset the apple cart," or "make waves." You could repeat the sad—and dangerous—words, so often heard: "But we've *always* done it this way."

But then you and your business would probably not improve, not progress, not prosper.

Every new product, every new advertising, marketing, and sales technique came from the mind's eye of a creative visionary, from the depths of the imagination of someone whose eyes opened to *really* see.

If not from insight and vision, tapping into the genius of creativity, from where else—in these last few generations alone—could have come trains and transistors, cars and computers, the telegraph, the telephone, and the television, airplanes and air conditioners, satellites and space stations, frozen food and fax machines?

You can have the vision you need to conceive and create.

When you open your eyes, you open your possibilities, and you visualize not only what already is but what can be.

No matter what you have already accomplished and become, you can always envision more.

For no matter how glorious the sunset, in the morning your eyes turn east—to the dawning of a new day—to new sights to see, new horizons to pursue.

Yet vision alone is not enough.

Vision can be no more than daydreams that disappear, no more than wisps of skywriting that drift away before the last word is finished.

Vision realized is imagination coupled with drive and determination, with courage and creativity, with sweat and hard work.

Sam Walton—acknowledged, before his recent death, to be the wealthiest man in America—did not accumulate his fortune just by dreaming of a chain of discount stores in rural communities. He worked incredibly hard—sixteen, eighteen, and twenty hours a day—planning, buying, selling, traveling, building, and, eventually, succeeding.

Steve Jobs and Steve Wozniak did not take on the world's business-machines giant with an "upstart" new product just by sitting in their garage with an idea for a new computer. They had unwavering and single-minded determination that drove them to meet every challenge, to overcome every obstacle, and to prevail against daunting odds.

Ben and Jerry didn't just envision a better-tasting ice cream. They had the convictions and the courage to decide to do business safely and cleanly, to share their gains with their coworkers and community, to make a commitment not only to product and profit but to principles of conscience.

The "American dream" starts with dreams and visions, but becomes reality through hard work and dogged determination.

You can have the tenacity to make your dreams real when you follow the advice of political activist Ann Stone: Be "the kind of person who gets in a rowboat to go after Moby Dick—and takes along the tartar sauce."

A word of caution.

Sometimes what you think you see really isn't there at all.

There was once a king who hired many laborers from the village to help build his grand new palace.

Every morning the workers came in through the palace gates, and every evening they left through the same gates.

The palace guards noticed that each evening, as they departed, the villagers pulled behind them little wooden wagons filled with sand. The guards were sure that the workers were stealing precious jewels from the castle and were hiding them in the sand of their wagons.

So each evening the guards checked every wagon carefully, trying to find what the villagers were hiding in the sand.

They found nothing, so they checked even more carefully until they were going through the sand grain by grain. Still, the guards could find no jewels—nothing that the peasants were taking.

The guards were totally baffled until they realized that the villagers were not stealing jewels from the castle. They were stealing little wooden wagons filled with sand.

And yet sometimes, when you think you see nothing, there is greatness right before your eyes.

Someone shoved a block of marble aside as useless.

Michelangelo said, "Bring it to my studio. An angel is imprisoned in that marble, and I intend to set it free."

You can be like those described as ones "who have eyes, but do not see," or you can see both your problems and your potential, your challenges and your capabilities—eye to eye.

Every waking moment you are bombarded with myriad sights and images.

Before long, everything that you see can seem to blend into one hodgepodge of color, shape, and texture. Even the keenest eye can be blurred. Even the clearest vision can become distorted.

So—even when it seems difficult—keep your dreams and your visions before you.

For "if you really, really want it, it is no dream."

Then see all your tomorrows open up right before your eyes—your tomorrows, with all your achievements and your successes; your goals realized and your visions fulfilled.

The Second Commandment

~

"DO NOT UTTER

A FALSE REPORT"

We all grew up hearing the legend about the "Father of our Country," George Washington, who chopped down the cherry tree and admitted his guilt with the famous phrase, "I cannot tell a lie."

It's good advice—even today.

Do you want your colleagues to respect you? Do you want your customers and competitors to believe you? Do you want everyone you know to have trust and faith in you?

Then always tell the truth. Let your word be your bond, and let your honor be your word.

It's good advice, but it's not always easy to follow.

Your coworker—or your boss, or your best customer—comes to you with a broad smile and a handful of snapshots. "Look. This is my new grandson. Isn't he the most beautiful baby you've ever seen?"

Truth be told, the baby looks like a million other babies, and really is a bit on the ugly side.

So what do you say?

Do you lie and say, "That sure is a beautiful baby! What a gorgeous face! What lovely eyes!"

Do you tell the truth, the whole truth—"What a plain-looking baby he is"—and risk insulting or offending?

Or can you find a way to say something that is truthful enough so that it will be heard as words of kindness and compliment?

You can say, "What a baby that is." "That's quite a grandson you have there." Or find one quality that you can sincerely praise. "He really has a full head of hair." "That's quite a chin—strong and firm—just like his grandpa's."

In doing so you tell the truth without compromising. You tell the truth without offending. You tell the truth, and you and the grandpa and that little baby are all happy.

But it's not always as simple as reacting to baby pictures.

Your boss says, "When Mr. Smith calls, tell him I'm not in."

You know that's not the truth. Your boss is sitting at his desk, working on some papers, or she is right down the hall in the conference room.

And now you've been instructed to join in a deception by telling Mr. Smith a lie—that your boss is not in.

It's not a very big lie; it probably isn't a very harmful lie. But, it is a lie, nevertheless. And you are uncomfortable about not telling the truth.

So what do you do?

You find words that send the message that your boss wants given—and may even convey reality in the "code words" that business people understand—without compromising your integrity, without telling a lie.

You can say, "I'm sorry, he's not available right now." You can say, "I'm sorry, she can't talk to you right now." You can say, "He can't be disturbed right now, but I'll be glad to take a message and tell him that you called."

Your words are true, your purpose is accomplished, your personal honor is preserved.

Speaking words of truth may be more delicate and more difficult when the speaker must be direct and forthright, and when the listener's personal and professional ego and self-esteem are at stake.

"How am I doing?" "Is my work satisfactory?" "Did my report cover all the bases?" "How was my presentation?" "Do you think I deserve a chance to head up the project?" "Do I have a future here?"

What do you say when the work is good, but not great? What do you say when performance is disappointing, when expectations are not realized, when the goals are not met? What do you say when failure is more likely than success?

You could equivocate. You could follow that sweet advice given in childhood: "If you can't say anything nice, don't say anything at all." You could use that popular conversational ploy and say, "Your presentation is so *interesting.* Your idea is so *intriguing.*" But, of course, you've accomplished *nothing,* because you've said *nothing.* Both you and the one to whom you are speaking know that your words are no more than a rhetorical ruse.

You could be brutally honest, telling it "like it is," telling "the truth, the whole truth, and nothing but the truth."

But you have to be very cautious. Remember that at least some of your truth comes not from a dispassionate, objective standard but through the prism of your background, your biases, your subjective judgments. What is "true" for you may not be "true" for everyone around you.

And then you need to be very, very careful. For your words have great power. Your words can doom dreams and destroy hope. Your words can humble and humiliate and crush the spirit. Your words can shatter worlds.

So how shall you best speak your words of truth—as frank and as painful as they may be?

Gently wrap your words of truth in words of kindness. Temper your criticism with praise, your admonition with comfort, your reality with reason. Use your words of truth to build up instead of tear down, to instruct, to encourage, to uplift. Give your words of truth as a gift of caring and of sharing.

Ultimately, you and the person to whom you are speaking—and your business—will benefit. For "words that are spoken from the heart enter into the heart."

Yet there are times when it would be so much easier—and so much more productive and profitable—to utter a false report.

You know that your product is inferior to another. Do you try to improve your goods, or do you try to bolster your sales with false claims and empty assurances?

You know that your product has a serious defect. Do you try to correct it—or remove the product from the market until the problem can be fixed—or do you pretend that you don't know and remain silent?

You know that your plant is spewing toxins into the nearby river. Do you shut down your plant, get rid of the poisons, and clean up the river, or do you change numbers and falsify reports?

You know that your customer's complaint is valid. Do you accept responsibility and try to correct the problem, or do you deny any wrongdoing and dispute the customer's claims?

Will you remain silent? Will you look the other way? Will you lie? Will you use your words to rationalize and make excuses, to deceive and defraud?

Or will you speak words of truth, regardless of outcome or consequence?

These are choices that can make or break you in business.

For at stake may be your job, your livelihood, your company, your career, your reputation, your report to the stockholders.

And these are the choices that can make or break you as a human being, for here you have to decide what is more important—your pocketbook or your principles, your convenience or your conscience?

Lies—like Pinocchio's nose—just keep getting bigger and bigger. One lie is never enough, for lies have a way of feeding on themselves and expanding. So once you lie, you usually have to keep on lying. And lying—though it may seem the easy way out—is really very hard. For when you lie, you have to remember what you said, whom you told, and what you told to whom. And most of all, you have to live in constant fear of being discovered—caught in your lie and exposed.

But the truth you have to tell only once.

How different history would have been had President Nixon simply called in the reporters one day after the break-in at Watergate and said, "A few dumb underlings from my campaign staff committed this stupid break-in. They thought they were going to help our campaign, and they thought they were acting on orders from people close to me. I take full responsibility for their foolish behavior, and I apologize to the Democratic National Committee and to the citizens of the United States. I am sorry that this sordid incident happened, but I promise you, nothing like it will ever happen again. I hope you will forgive me and the members of my campaign staff."

The truth would have been painful to speak; honestly admitting guilt would have been hard to do. It would have hurt the president in the eyes of the American people, and his reputation and his standing in the polls might have suffered for a little while. But in a matter of weeks—probably in a matter of days—the whole incident would have been forgotten by a forgiving public.

Instead, the president piled lie on top of lie, because once he started with his falsehoods, he got so caught up lying that he himself probably no longer knew the difference between truth and fiction. His lies caused the country a "national nightmare" and cost him the presidency.

A lie may seem to save you at the moment, but eventually your lies will ruin you. For no matter what their immediate benefit, lies follow you and hound you, mock you and torment you, haunt you and give you no rest.

Ultimately, no matter what the momentary cost—and it may be enormous if your job, your company's profits, your ability to put food on your table, is at stake—"the truth will set you free." Your pride and your integrity will be preserved, and you will be able to sleep at night.

A day, a week, or a year from now, whatever hurtful consequence may have occurred from telling the truth will be long forgotten. But the satisfaction, the deep joy, and the inner peace that you feel will remain with you always.

So always tell the truth, because the words you speak ripple into eternity and resound throughout the universe until the end of time.

There is another kind of false report that we all too often utter that brings pain and hurt and can cause irreparable damage—words that are a violation of confidence, of privacy, of trust, of decency.

"Did you know?" "Did you hear?" "Wait until you hear this." "Can you keep a secret?" "Do I have something to tell you." "I promised I wouldn't say a word, but I know that I can trust you. So if you promise you won't tell a soul, listen to this."

Rumors, scuttlebutt, idle chatter, and frivolous chitchat often seem to be the lifeblood of the company grapevine. Often, more time is spent fanning gossip than on doing the job.

But gossip and slander are not victimless crimes. Words do not just dissipate into midair. Words can swirl around, taking on lives of their own, affronting and harassing, causing embarrassment and harm.

The childhood verse is so very wrong: "Sticks and stones may break my bones, but words can never hurt me."

Wrong.

Words *can* injure and damage, maim and destroy—forcefully, painfully, lastingly—as surely as a sharp sword or a piercing arrow.

Plans have been disrupted, deals have been lost, companies have fallen, because of idle gossip or malicious slander. Reputations have been sullied, careers have been ruined, lives have been devastated, because of cruel lies or vicious rumors.

Even the most benign comment, the seemingly innocuous remark, the slightly veiled innuendo, the most innocent of gossip, can do great damage and harm.

Your words have such power to do good or evil that they must be chosen carefully, wisely, and well.

For once evil words have passed your lips, they can never be retrieved.

It once happened that a man came to a rabbi and said, "Oh, Rabbi, I have done wrong. I have slandered my friend. I have told lies about him. I have spread rumors. But now I am sorry for what I have done and what I have said.

"I've gone to my friend to tell him how sorry I am and to ask his forgiveness. And out of the goodness of his heart, he has forgiven me. But now I have to seek forgiveness from God for breaking His commandments. So I've come to you, my teacher, to ask: How can I be forgiven by God for slandering and gossiping about my friend?"

The rabbi looked thoughtfully at the man, and then he asked, "Do you see that feather pillow over there on my bed? Take that pillow and go into the center of town, into the town square, and cut the pillow open and let all the feathers fly to the wind. That will be your punishment for what you have done, for the ill words you have spoken."

The man was quite puzzled by the rabbi's instruction, but he did just as he was told. He took the feather pillow to the center of town, cut it open, and watched the feathers fly away in the wind.

Then he returned to the rabbi and said, "I've done just as you told me. I took the feather pillow to the center of town, cut it open, and watched the feathers fly to the wind. Now am I forgiven for slandering and gossiping about my friend?"

The rabbi replied, "No, you are not forgiven yet. For you have fulfilled only half your task. First you let the feathers fly to the wind. Now go out and collect every feather that flew away."

The words you speak echo forever.

Not only can you help wipe out the pain caused by gossip and rumors by not spreading them yourself, but you can also choose not to listen to them.

It takes at least two people to sustain gossip and rumor, to prolong the life of evil words that fly away and cannot be retrieved—the speaker *and* the listener. Even if you never breathe a word of what you hear to another living soul, if you eagerly await hearing a juicy tidbit of gossip, you become a participant in the rumor-mongering. You provide the place where rumors are heard, where they are passed on, where they flourish and grow. But if you refuse to listen—which takes great strength of character, but that's what we're talking about here, isn't it?—then the gossip and the rumors can die a well-deserved death.

By being neither a speaker nor a listener, you help sustain the honor of another human being, and you bring a touch more decency to your office, to your business, to your world.

It has been said that great people talk about ideas, ordinary people talk about things, and small, petty people talk about people.

You can be a great person if you cherish another's name and reputation as if it were your own. You can be a great person when you speak kind, gentle words—words that continually support and uplift and praise.

You can be a great person when the words of your mouth are ever-acceptable words of goodness and worth; when decency and dignity are your guides, and truth is your constant companion.

The Third Commandment

~

"DO NO

UNRIGHTEOUSNESS

IN WEIGHTS

AND MEASURES"

The story is told that when Abraham Lincoln was a young boy, he was a clerk in a small dry-goods store. One day, when he realized that he had overcharged a customer, he walked two miles through the snow to immediately return the overcharge—one penny.

A recent cartoon vividly illustrates how different the response has become in our day: The customer pays with a ten-dollar bill, but after she leaves the store, the storekeeper realizes that he has received not a ten-dollar bill, but rather a hundred-dollar bill. Now he has a real moral dilemma: Shall he tell his partner?

Your measure as a human being—and your reputation, success, or failure in the world of business—is often determined by how accurately you measure, how meticulously you count, how honestly you deal.

It is, in reality, ever so easy to cheat. A thumb on the scale makes the product cost more—and the profit greater. Inaccurately counted change puts extra pennies into the cash register. Skimpy cutting of the cloth makes the dress just a little tight—the customer won't really notice, will she?—but provides enough extra material to make a blouse—and more money. "Creative accounting" keeps the books looking good, but saves a lot of taxes.

And, after all, whom can it hurt?

"This guy doesn't know anything about cars. Let's tell him we put in a new air filter. He'll never know the difference."

"My company is so big that it will never miss this pencil and these paper clips that I'm taking home."

"My corporation is so rich that it can't possibly be affected by the few personal long-distance calls I make."

"I work plenty hard around here, so why shouldn't I take a longer lunch hour today—and tomorrow, and the next day?"

"No one will count this order when it arrives. So what if one box is missing? My kid can really use these new sneakers."

A penny here, an hour there, a phone call here, an ounce or two there, hardly seems like cheating. After all, we tell ourselves, *everyone* does it, and no one really gets hurt, and it's not as if I'm being really dishonest, because it's just little things—and little things don't make a difference.

Or do they?

When I was about eight or nine years old, many new houses were being built in my neighborhood on the old southeast side of Chicago. Every day after school, after the workmen had left, all the kids in the neighborhood would gather at the new homesites to run and jump and play in the big piles of dirt, in the (to us) deep excavations, and to climb up, around, and into the frames of the houses that were being built.

One day a gigantic stack of bright red bricks was piled up at the building site. Those bricks were so hefty, so smooth, so fire-engine red, so wonderful, that I—and all the other kids—just had to have one. So all of us—maybe ten or twelve kids—took home a heavy red brick.

It never even occurred to me that taking a brick might be a problem. After all, there were hundreds, probably thousands, of bricks in that pile. Nobody would miss a few bricks. And besides, they were so great that I just *had* to have one.

My parents saw the bricks through different eyes. "It's stealing," my father said. "You stole someone else's property."

"You'll have to return that brick," my mother said. "And it is not enough to just go put it back on the pile. First thing tomorrow morning, before you go to school, you take that brick back, give it to the workman, and apologize for taking his brick."

"But," I protested, "it's only *one* brick. They'll never even know it's gone, and it won't make any difference to them anyway. It's only *one* brick."

My father listened quietly, and then he said, "You're right, it's only one brick. But how many of you took only one brick?"

"Ten or twelve of us," I said.

"Ah," sighed my father. "Now it's not just one brick, but ten or twelve. And how many bricks were in that pile?"

I thought up the biggest number I could possibly imagine. "There were a hundred hundred thousand bricks," I said. "See, they won't miss just one."

And then my father asked the fundamental question: "What if," he asked, "a hundred hundred thousand kids took just one brick?"

Finally, I understood. If everyone took just one brick, there would be no big pile of bricks, no new houses built with bright red brick walls.

There's very little difference between the little kid who took just one red brick all those years ago and the person today who makes just one extra phone call, who puts just one little thumb on the scale, or who takes home just one little pencil or one pair of sneakers.

Dishonesty is dishonesty, and cheating is cheating, whether it involves a little or a lot. If you cheat, if you defraud, you diminish yourself as a human being, and you violate the trust that others have in you.

And eventually, you will pay.

Even if you do not get caught, your gains are somebody else's losses. And you can be sure that those losses will be made up—passed on to you as a consumer—by higher prices on the shelves, higher fees for services, higher costs for everything you buy.

But you will pay with more than money.

If you cheat, if your weights and measures are inaccurate, if your financial dealings are shoddy, if you take things that do not belong to you, you won't be able to hide it forever. People *will* find out. Then your reputation and your business will suffer, because people don't want to deal with someone who can't be trusted.

Not long ago, I took my car in for repairs. I was given a cost estimate for the work that was to be done, and when the mechanic found additional work that needed doing, he called me and carefully explained the problem, his recommendation, and the added cost. When I came to pick up my car, it seemed as if everything had been done in a thorough and professional manner.

But soon after I drove the car off the mechanic's lot, I

realized that more than half a tank of gas had been drained from the gas tank.

After spending hundreds of dollars for repairs, I had been ripped off for a few dollars' worth of gas. Unheard of? Maybe. But it happened.

Did the mechanic think that I was so stupid that I wouldn't notice? Did he think that I wouldn't mind? Did he really think he could get away with it?

Surely that is the last time I will ever use that mechanic. And at least five or ten dozen of my "closest and most intimate friends"—that is, anyone within hearing distance of my voice—will hear the story of what happened at that garage.

That mechanic's ill-gotten gain will cost him more than he could have ever hoped to get.

That's the price of dishonest dealing.

And your dishonest dealings will come to haunt you, for you will have to live with them for a long, long time.

Once there was a king who engaged a certain carpenter to build houses for the people of his kingdom. The carpenter built house after house, and the people who lived in the houses—and the king—were very pleased.

To show his gratitude for the carpenter's fine work, the king asked him to build more and more houses, for which the king paid more and more money. The carpenter was busy building house after house, and he became increasingly wealthy from the generous fees that the king paid.

One day the carpenter said to himself, "The king is paying me very handsomely to build these houses. Yet I am the only one who knows the fine quality of the materials that I use to build the houses and how much time and effort it takes to build each one. I think that from now on, I will continue to make the outside of the houses look just as beautiful as always, but on the inside of the houses—in the parts that most people will never see—I will use materials that don't cost as much. The houses will seem to be just as good as before, the king will continue to pay me the same fee for each house, but because of all the money I save by buying materials that aren't as good as the original materials, I will make much more money on each house, and I will become richer and richer."

And that is exactly what the carpenter did. The houses he built still looked wonderful on the outside, but because he used second-class materials on the inside, the houses weren't as sturdy or as strong as before. Yet he became a very wealthy man, because the king was still paying for a first-class job.

One day the king asked the carpenter to visit the palace. The king said, "You have done such a fine job building such beautiful houses for my kingdom that I now want to give you a very special task. I have decided to have you build the finest house you have ever built. Make this the very best house in the whole kingdom, second only to my palace. Spare no expense; the entire treasury of my kingdom is open to you to pay for the costs of this house. I have great plans for this house, and I want it to be the most magnificent house anyone has ever seen."

The carpenter was overjoyed with this assignment. Here was his chance to get all the money he could ever want. He built the fanciest house he could imagine—fancy on the outside. But on the inside, he used second- and third- and fourth-rate materials. He worked quickly and sloppily, with little regard for workmanship or pride. Yet he took more and more money from the king's treasury, as if he were buying the finest materials and employing world-class craftsmen.

The house was finished—and the carpenter had become a very, very rich man from all the money he had taken from the treasury but had not spent on the materials or the construction of the house.

The day came when he was to turn over the key to the house to the king. The king called together all his servants and many, many people from throughout the kingdom, for this was, indeed, a very special house, and the king had a very special purpose for it in mind.

The king said, "For years my friend the carpenter has been building beautiful houses for the people of my kingdom, but he has never lived in one of the houses he has built. This house is his finest creation—he worked harder on this house than on any other; no expense was spared in making it the finest house in the kingdom. So to show my gratitude to the carpenter for all that he has done for me and for my kingdom during all these years, I give him this—the very best house he has ever built—as a gift to live in for the rest of his days.

And the carpenter had to live in the house he had built for the rest of his life.

This might be just a fanciful story if something very similar had not just happened in real life.

Habitat for Humanity, the group that builds houses for the poor—and has come to national attention through the personal involvement of former President and Mrs. Jimmy Carter—built twenty-seven low-cost houses in Dade County, Florida. Some of these houses—built entirely by hand by volunteers—were right in the path of Hurricane Andrew, which devastated South Florida in the late summer of 1992. Yet almost every house built by the Habitat for Humanity volunteers survived the destructive forces of the hurricane's winds and rains. On one street, the only houses whose roofs remained were the houses built by the group. The leader of the Greater Miami Habitat for Humanity chapter said simply, "We didn't cut corners when we built them."

In the end honesty pays.

But most important, you will suffer for your dishonesty with the loss of your own peace of mind.

To paraphrase the modern prayer by Rabbi Sidney Greenberg, "Take heed how you live by day, lest fear of discovery haunt your sleep and rob you of the peace you crave." In the dark of the night, you have to answer to yourself. And no matter how much you rationalize, or how many excuses you invent, you know whether or not you have done right.

How much can you enjoy money that you know is not rightfully yours? How much can you rejoice in the "fruits of your labors" when you know you have come by them dishonestly?

A well-known financier—who would eventually get caught up in the scandals that rocked Wall Street in the late 1980s—thought that he could assuage his conscience by giving some of what he knew was his ill-gotten gain to a wide variety of charitable causes. In one of his most magnanimous gifts, he endowed a large public building.

In gratitude for his gift, the institution carved the name of this benefactor and his wife into the stone archway at the entrance to the building.

When his devious financial practices became known—as, inevitably, they would—the institution was greatly embarrassed that their building—built with funds obtained in fraudulent transactions—carried the name of the supposed benefactor, whose gift was of money that was really not his to give.

The institution could have demolished the building that was already built. But that would have done little good, for it had no way of determining whose money it had really spent, nor any way of returning money to rightful owners. So the institution did the only thing it could do.

One day the so-called financier-benefactor stood on the sidewalk—quietly weeping—watching as the institution sandblasted his name off the building.

His dishonesty had caught up with him, causing him not only sleepless nights and, eventually, years in prison, but public shame and ridicule, and a self-inflicted infamous name that will follow him to the grave.

The scriptural law demanding accuracy in weights and measures—complete honesty in the world of commerce—was taken so seriously that in olden times, the rabbi of the city would go from business to business checking the scale weights used by the merchants. The rabbi's certification that the weights and measures were accurate and correct assured the buyers that they were not being cheated, and created a marketplace atmosphere of confidence and trust.

In modern times a number of companies have gone to great lengths to create that same kind of trust.

For example, companies that sell cereals and crackers have begun to place a modern-day certification of weights and measures on the boxes of their products for all to read.

Company honesty was called into question when cereal boxes looked only partially full. People thought they were being cheated. So now, many boxes carry a statement: "This package is sold by weight and not by volume. When it was packed, it was as full as practical without damage to contents. Occasionally, a package may not appear full due to settling of contents during delivery and handling."

Thus, the company says: "It is not enough that *we* are sure that what we are doing is proper and right. *You*—our customer—must believe in us and have confidence in us. Since appearances may deceive—package contents may settle in shipping causing the box to look only partially full—we are telling you right up front that you are getting full measure for the price you pay. We are putting that guarantee right on our box, and we are staking our reputation—and your continued patronage—on telling you the truth."

What created marketplace confidence in ancient times works just as well today.

Yet honest dealings in the modern marketplace often require much more subtlety and much more finesse than a package label can provide.

Do you remember back to second or third grade? What was one of the first lessons your teachers taught you? "Do your own work. Don't look over at anyone else's paper. No copying." And then in fifth or sixth grade, the lesson became even more powerful: "Never call anyone else's work your own. Quote your sources. When you use material written by another, make sure you give credit to the author. Otherwise, it's plagiarism."

Old school lessons take on an unusual complexity in the everyday world of business.

Whose idea is it? Who made the suggestion? Who created the plan? Who offered the proposal?

To be sure, ideas bubble up from many people and places, and are often improved and refined by teamwork in meetings, conferences, seminars, and casual conversation. But do you steal someone else's idea and make it your own, or do you give credit where—and to whom—credit is due?

The "product of the mind" is as real as the product of the assembly line. "Intellectual property" is as valuable as tangible property. Taking an idea that does not belong to you is as wrong—and as harmful—as taking a thing that does not belong to you.

Ideas—and their creators—need and deserve your honesty and your honor.

And they need your respectful protection. For modern technology has made it so very easy to take someone else's ideas, words, melodies, or images. In seconds a photocopy machine can make copies of pages of a book. In minutes a tape deck can make a copy of an audiotape, a VCR can make a copy of a movie, a hard drive can make a copy of a computer disk.

"You'll love this music. I'll make a copy of it at home tonight and bring it to you tomorrow." "Here are the journal articles for you to read. I just ran them off on the machine." "Hey, I hear you have the newest computer program. Can you make me a copy?" Electronic copying has become so commonplace that few of us give it a second thought.

Yet copying is copying. It is taking something that belongs to another and calling it your own.

It may seem as if little harm is being done, especially since "everyone does it," yet what is really at stake—besides the personal question of honesty and integrity—is someone's livelihood. If you copy a $9.95 cassette, or a $19.95 book, or a $29.95 movie, or a $499.95 computer program, it means that the maker of the product—and all the other people involved in the project—don't receive fair compensation. You are using their product—and their collective creativity—without paying.

Ancient law put it very simply: "Do not violate another's boundaries" by crossing over into another's land, fields, or crops to take something that does not belong to you, infringing on rights and jeopardizing livelihood.

Today, "boundaries" are much more complex, for they are not just fences on land, but they include ideas, creativity, production, and product; they include books and tapes and computer programs.

But the principle remains the same.

Don't take *anything* that does not belong to you, for it impinges on another's property, it violates another's rights, it may "take money out of another's pocket."

When you respect and protect the work of another's mind and hands, you help insure another human being's rights and dignity, and you help make the business world a safer and more secure place for everyone—you, too—to be and to create, to risk and to succeed.

And for completely honest dealing in the marketplace, ask yourself the hardest question: How much is your integrity worth? What is the price tag on your soul?

There will be those who seek your favor. There will be those who come to influence you. There will be those who try to sway you. There will be those who want to control you.

They will come in all guises: They will be blatant and brazen; they will be clever and crafty; they will be sophisticated and subtle.

They will offer prestige, power, possessions.

In your specialty store or boutique, what do you say to the salesman who says, "If you would consider giving my product more shelf space—say, six rows of display instead of the two you have now—I'd like to give you this great company T-shirt to wear"? Or what do you say if the offer is not of a T-shirt, but of tickets to the baseball game, or of a television set, or of a trip to Hawaii?

In arranging your shelves, will the promise of a gift—or shall we call it a bribe?—influence your decision? Is displaying more of the product really in your store's best interest, or are you doing it in exchange for the promised prize? Will you rearrange your shelves for a T-shirt? If not for a T-shirt, then how about for that trip to Hawaii?

Do you have a price?

If you take the gift, to whom does it really belong—to you, or to your company, which is paying for the product? If you take the gift, do you tell your boss, or hope that no one will find out—until, of course, the salesman's boss calls your boss and asks, "Say, how did you like that television set we sent over to you last week?"

What if you are the one offering the gift? Are you simply showing your appreciation, or are you trying to bribe the customer? Are you using an accepted business practice of offering incentives, or are you using undue influence and pressure?

The question is not just for the sales floor, but for the office and the executive suite as well. Who gets the Frequent Flyer miles earned for taking airplane flights: the employee who takes the trip or the company that pays for the ticket? If you get the mileage for your personal use, will you make your reservation on the most direct route, on the least expensive airline, or will you use your favorite airline—where you already have the most miles accumulated toward your own summer vacation plans—regardless of convenience or cost to your company?

What about all the Christmas gifts that are sent from business to business every year? Are they sincere expressions of appreciation and affection, or are they intended to influence future decisions and prejudice future choices?

Gifts can be lovely tokens of gratitude and fondness. But gifts can blind the eye and confuse the mind.

Marketplace gifts—given or received—can lead to false expectations and mistaken assumptions, to favoritism and bias, to mistrust, anger, and turmoil.

So to maintain the integrity of the marketplace, the pressure on each individual to make personal choices and difficult decisions about giving or receiving gifts can be replaced by creating a collective company conscience.

Every business can create its own gift policy. If gifts are to be given—to employees or customers—as incentives for better production or more business, then the gift policy will outline the requirements, the achievements, and the rewards. If gifts are to be accepted—in the normal course of business, or for a certain level of selling or buying, or as holiday favors—then, the gift policy will spell out who may take the gift, and who gets to keep the gift. The gift policy will also delineate who keeps and uses the Frequent Flyer miles or any other reward that is earned while doing business on behalf of the company.

A clearly articulated policy removes doubt and indecision about what is permitted and what is prohibited, what is acceptable and what is questionable. Few can object—and fewer will get themselves or their companies into legal or ethical trouble—when the policy is clearly made and equally applied. Everyone simply wants to know what is fair and what is right, and having a company policy will accomplish exactly that.

A few hours or days of company time used to create policy will bring the whole marketplace a long way toward solving one of its ongoing dilemmas, and will help avoid personal distress and professional heartache.

The modern marketplace is full of opportunity to cheat and to steal, to "look the other way" at dishonesty and deceit, to profit from ill-gotten gain.

But when you do what is right *because it is right,* when you measure accurately and count exactly, when you are scrupulous in your commerce and meticulous in your dealings, then your colleagues will respect you, your customers and competitors will believe you, and everyone will trust you.

And ultimately you will succeed, for everyone likes to deal with an honest man, everyone wants to do business with an honest woman.

In the Old West, there was no greater compliment than "He's as honest as the day is long."

Even today—especially today—there is still no greater tribute: Your honesty speaks your praise.

The Fourth Commandment

~

"LOVE YOUR

NEIGHBOR

AS YOURSELF"

Moshe Leib, the late-eighteenth-century rabbi of the little Ukrainian town of Sasov, taught: "From a peasant, I learned to love."

The man was sitting at an inn, eating and drinking with other peasants. For a very, very long time, he was silent. Then he turned to one of the men sitting near him, and he asked, "Tell me, do you love me?"

The other peasant replied, "Of course. I love you very much."

The peasant was silent again for a very, very long time. Then, he turned to his friend and said, "You say that you love me, but you do not know what I need. If you really loved me, you would know." And again, he was silent.

Rabbi Moshe said, "I understood. To know the needs of other human beings, to feel their joy and to bear the burdens of their sorrow—that is true love."

How can you know the needs of another human being? How can you feel someone else's pain or share another's happiness?

Ancient Scripture put it most succinctly: "Love your neighbor as yourself."

Treat every human being as you want to be treated—with understanding, with fairness, with kindness, and with compassion. Give everyone else the same decency and dignity, the same honesty and integrity, the same warmth and concern that *you* want.

All of life, and surely all of business—whatever your business or profession, product or service—is *people relating to people:* employers, employees, colleagues, coworkers, clients, and customers.

And the *art of doing business* depends on how you treat each and every person who comes your way.

The popular myth is that "nice guys finish last." The big lie is that in order to succeed, you can't let personal feelings get in the way; you have to be "hard-nosed" and "cutthroat."

In reality it is neither your "nose" nor your "throat" that counts, but another part of your face. The old bumper sticker tells it all: "If someone needs a smile, give him one of yours."

Being aloof, gruff, or stern never got anyone anywhere. Who wants to be treated like that? Certainly not you. And surely not the people you meet.

When you begin with a big smile and a good word, when you are warm and friendly, when you are open and sincere, you convey respect and regard; you build goodwill and trust; you create an atmosphere where anything—and everything—is possible.

But sometimes you forget. Sometimes *getting* the job done becomes more important than *why* the job is being done in the first place. Sometimes you think that *what* you are selling is more important than *to whom* you are selling.

Not long ago I was waiting for a table in a very crowded restaurant. A young couple, holding hands and looking very much in love, walked in. The young man said, "We'd like a table for two, please."

The hassled hostess hardly looked up from her reservation book. She just curtly said, "We're not taking any walk-ins tonight." The young couple looked rather stunned and, without saying another word, turned and walked out—most likely never to return to that restaurant again.

How much nicer—and how much better for business—it would have been if the hostess had cared not just about the bodies that were filling her tables but about the *people* who wanted to sit at those tables.

Then she might have said, "Oh, I am so very sorry. We've had so many diners tonight that we just don't have any more tables available. We're booked solid for the next three hours, and I am so sorry that we won't be able to accommodate you. But thank you so much for coming in. I hope that you'll come back again soon. And when you do, I'd like you to have some complimentary appetizers. Here's a rain check, a coupon good for when you come back, to receive your appetizers on the house."

That couple would have been back—maybe even the very next night—and would have told all their friends about the warm, friendly reception they had received.

Like a product or a store, and you'll tell *four* friends. *Dislike* the way you were treated, and you'll tell *twelve* friends.

A can of string beans is the same can of string beans at every grocery store on the block. Where will you buy your string beans? Most likely, you'll shop in the store that couples its string beans with warm, friendly service.

It's the same in the office, the lab, the factory. Employees and coworkers are more productive, more loyal—satisfied and happy—when they are treated fairly, decently, and with dignity than when they are used and taken for granted, when they feel like no more than a tiny cog in a giant corporate wheel.

There is little worse than going to work and feeling used or abused, underutilized or unappreciated, picked on, put down, or powerless. There is little more that cripples American business as much as personality conflicts that disrupt the workplace and diminish people, as well as production and profit.

In recent years many companies have instituted a wide variety of programs intended to respect and value—and gain the most from—each and every individual.

Some companies have used variations of the Japanese concept of teamwork, utilizing team goal setting, shared responsibility, and shared achievement, complete with team uniforms and team cheers.

Some companies have taken to calling each employee an "associate," conveying a sense of partnership, engendering allegiance and loyalty.

Some companies have made every employee a small part owner of the business. So you can now rent a car from one of the owners of the rental car company, who will presumably take better care of customers because of pride of ownership. Or you can get the very best possible deal from the appliance store because talking to your salesman—who is not an hourly worker, but an owner—is "like having an uncle in the business."

Some new "start-up" companies—especially a number of high-tech firms and mail-order-catalog companies—have started from scratch by throwing away all previous assumptions and creating new ways to do business. These kinds of

companies invite full participation of every single worker—
from top management to the person who sweeps the floor at
the end of the day—in every phase of design, production, and
sales. Each member of the team contributes ideas and hard
work. Each is respected and valued by the other; each has
equal voice and equal vote; each feels a sense of responsibility,
commitment, and personal investment. The results of this
kind of business concept are products that have been hailed
for their quality and price, companies that are admired for
their service, and workers who feel pride in achievement and
reap the benefits of success.

Each one of these concepts—and the hundreds of others
like them being tried and tested throughout the business
world—is a recognition of fundamental truths: the intrinsic
worth and value of *each* human being; the absolute equality of
every human being.

Loving your neighbor as yourself, treating each person as
you want to be treated, creates a work world where everyone
feels worthy, valued, and empowered; where nobody has to
lose so that somebody else can win.

In that kind of work world, people thrive. And when
people thrive, business soars.

Loving your neighbor as yourself isn't hard when you remember that he, that she, is just like you.

You want a fair deal, an honest price, don't you? So do your
suppliers, your customers, your clients.

You like recognition and praise for your ideas and achievements, don't you? So does every coworker and colleague.

You want a good income and equal pay for equal work,
don't you? So does every worker in your company.

You want time off when an emergency arises in your personal life, don't you? So does everyone who has to go to the
doctor or tend to a sick child.

You need full and fair benefits to assure health care in illness and dignity in old age for you and your family, don't you? So does everyone.

You don't want an arbitrarily placed "glass ceiling" to keep you from advancement or promotion, do you? Neither does any woman or any member of any minority group who works for you.

You would like your fair share of the profits your company earns, wouldn't you? So does every single person who helped make those profits.

Loving your neighbor as yourself means that everyone benefits, everyone gains, everyone wins. That's what life—and business—is all about.

And loving your neighbor as yourself means that *you* benefit.

A passenger was standing in line at an airline ticket counter, listening to the person at the front of the line berate the ticket clerk. The man was yelling, screaming, pounding his fist, and making one demand after another, one threat after another.

Finally, the furious customer left the counter, and our passenger reached the head of the line.

He said to the ticket clerk, "I want to compliment you. That other passenger was horrible to you; he said terrible things to you; he was mean and nasty. But through it all you never lost your smile, you never became angry. You were calm and polite. I really admire how you handled yourself."

"Thank you, sir," the clerk said. "I really appreciate your kind words. But don't worry. It's all right."

"How can it be all right?" the passenger asked. "That man was positively abusive to you. How can it be all right?"

And the ticket clerk said, "It's all right because, you see, that man is going to Cleveland. But his luggage is going to Singapore."

~

Every day you deal with scores of people who—literally or figuratively—can send your luggage to Singapore.

Why belittle? Why antagonize? Why create ill will?

No one benefits—certainly not you.

When you treat people kindly and politely, decently and with respect, there is a good chance that you and your "luggage" will wind up at the same place, at the same time.

What happens if you are the one who is being treated unfairly, the one who is being discriminated against, the one who is belittled or verbally abused? What if your boss takes advantage of you or your supervisor picks on you? What if going to work every day becomes a misery or, worse, a living nightmare? What if you can't quit because you need the money, but you don't know how you can continue because they are driving you crazy?

What do you do? Where do you turn?

You can seek advice and counsel from coworkers. You can "go through channels," asking for help from people up the line of authority. You can ask for a transfer, a new assignment, a new account to service. You can seek relief and redress, hoping that fairness and justice will prevail, that evil will be identified and punished, and that goodness will be recognized and rewarded. Or if all else fails, you can move on, knowing that your self-esteem and peace of mind are worth more than any job, and that your record and reputation will lead your new job search in the right directions.

You know that ultimately you cannot control others. And yet you know, just as strongly, that you can always control yourself.

When you are confronted by unpleasant, angry faces, you can still smile. When you are spoken to harshly, you can still reply sweetly. When erratic and irrational demands are made of you, you can still act rationally and calmly. When hateful words are spewed at you, you can still respond with love.

It is not simply a matter of "turning the other cheek." It is not simply knowing, with the philosopher Nietzsche, that "that which does not kill me makes me stronger." It is, rather, knowing that love for one another—profound human connection and concern—is the greatest good and the highest goal. When you continue to love, you render hate utterly powerless.

And except for the most hardened of nasty people, few will be able to resist your smile and your good cheer forever. With your continuing warmth and enthusiasm, you can dissipate the ill will that poisons your work world. In its place you can bring reconciliation and healing.

Yet there will be times when, no matter how much you desire it, how desperately you try, you will just not be able to influence or change horrible people and painful situations.

It is then that you are reminded that even people captured and enslaved, even people bound and shackled, even people in the darkest and most unassailable of prisons, always, always have *minds* that are free.

I know a woman who, as a young girl, was taken to a Nazi death camp. She watched as her townspeople were led off toward the gas chambers. Her nostrils were filled with the stench of bodies being burned in the crematoria. And on the very night that she knew that her mother was murdered, she was forced to dress in fine clothes and dance a delicate ballet for the pleasure of the camp commander.

How did she—and thousands of others—survive?

Psychotherapist Dr. Viktor Frankl, himself a Holocaust survivor, teaches, "...even in such terrible conditions of psychic and physical stress...man can preserve a vestige of spiritual freedom, of independence of mind....Everything can be taken from a man but one last thing: the last of human freedoms—*to choose one's attitude in a given set of circumstances, to choose one's own way.*"

It is admittedly almost obscene to use the horrific Nazi death camps to illustrate a modern-day business dilemma. No workplace trauma can come within light-years of the horrors of the concentration camps, the bamboo huts of the Vietnam POWs, the gulags of the old Soviet Union.

Yet from the survivors of those gruesome places, we learn important lessons that translate everywhere within the human condition. We learn to confront our own travails with free minds, choosing not to despair, but to endure; not to suffer, but to prevail; not to hate, but to love.

Do you remember the campus slogan of the sixties: "What if they gave a war and nobody came?"

If your work world declares "war" on you, you don't have to come. Instead you can be the messenger of peace and the transmitter of love.

Loving your neighbor means recognizing and appreciating the unique contribution that each and every person has to make to you and your business.

Regardless of age, regardless of experience, regardless of gender, regardless of physical challenge, regardless of color or creed, everyone—*everyone*—has something to give, and something to teach.

With youth comes idealism and enthusiasm.

With age comes wisdom and experience.

With men and women come point of view and know-how.

With physical challenge comes determination and tenacity.

With color and creed come diversity and awareness.

It does not matter how young or how old people are, or how much experience they have had. Everyone has something to offer you and your business, because success can come at any age.

William Pitt the younger was twenty-four when he became

prime minister of Great Britain. Golda Meir was seventy-one when she became prime minister of Israel.

Mozart was seven when he first began composing. George Bernard Shaw was ninety-two when his last full-length play was produced.

Joan of Arc, French heroine and Roman Catholic saint, was nineteen when she died. Mary Baker Eddy was directing the Christian Science Church at age eighty-nine.

Benjamin Franklin was only sixteen when he became a regular newspaper columnist, but he was eighty-one when he forged the compromise that framed the Constitution of the United States.

Bill Gates was barely out of his teens when he created Microsoft, now the largest software company in the world.

Ray Kroc was a middle-aged milk-shake-machine salesman when he started McDonald's, the fast-food hamburger chain that now circles the globe.

John Sculley had a distinguished tenure as president of Pepsi-Cola before making a midcareer change to become CEO of Apple Computer.

Lee Iacocca was the father of the ever-popular Mustang at Ford Motor Company before he went on to even greater accomplishments as the CEO of Chrysler Corporation.

Dr. A. Bartlett Giamatti had already been president of Yale University, president of the National League, and commissioner of Major League Baseball before his untimely death when he was only fifty-one years old. What more could one man hope to achieve in one lifetime—except length of days?

Dr. Linus Pauling, winner of two Nobel Prizes, continued to research and experiment, making significant contributions to the world of science and medicine well into his eighties.

And George Burns, who won an Academy Award when he was eighty, was still delighting audiences in his nineties.

And it does not matter how much success or failure or challenge people have already experienced. Everyone has something to offer you and your business, because out of the ashes
of failure can come new success, and from early triumph can
come even greater achievement.

Thomas Edison and Andrew Carnegie never graduated
from grade school. Wilbur Wright and Henry Ford dropped
out of high school.

Ludwig van Beethoven, partially deaf by his thirties and
totally deaf by his late forties, wrote his greatest music in the
last years of his life.

Abraham Lincoln lost three elections before he became the
president who saved a nation.

In 1899 Charles Duell, the director of the United States
Patent Office, said, "Everything that can be invented has already been invented."

And in the late 1920s Harry Warner, president of Warner
Brothers Pictures, said, "Who would ever want to hear movie
actors talk?"

Before going on to become a shipping magnate and one of
the world's richest men, Aristotle Onassis was a telephone
operator.

Fried chicken franchise king Colonel Sanders once sold in-
surance.

Forced into bankruptcy when his Laugh-O-Gram Corporation failed because of problems with the distributors of his
animated fairy tales, Walt Disney later became the most famous of all animators and head of one of the world's most
successful entertainment corporations.

Author Richard Bach received more than twenty rejection
slips for his fable *Jonathan Livingston Seagull* before it was
published and went on to become an international best-seller.

A crippling muscle disease has forced Barbara Jordan to

retire from Congress. Yet with her brilliant, facile mind she remains a renowned scholar and teacher of constitutional law, and a passionate advocate of social justice.

After shaky beginnings, including rowdy college days and taking over a faltering family business, Ted Turner's vision, determination, and grit have forever changed the face of news gathering and entertainment distribution.

And from the remains of the buy-out of his Fed-Mart stores, Sol Price created Price Club, the prototype warehouse-discount store, now being replicated by dozens of companies throughout the nation.

Abraham Joshua Heschel, a great mystic and teacher of our time, asked, "Who am I? A mere chip from the block of being? Am I not both the marble and the chisel? Being and foreseeing? Being and bringing into being?"

In each and every person—young and old, male and female, the veteran and the rookie—is both the raw material and the artist, the marble and the chisel, the reality and the potential.

Your business will best succeed and flourish when you take advantage of what each and every person can offer to you; when you listen and learn from both the wisdom of age and the enthusiasm of youth, from every point of view, from every experience, from every encounter, from everyone.

That's loving—and being loved and enriched by—your neighbor.

The story is told that long, long ago, in the land of Israel, lived two brothers who loved each other very, very much. The younger brother had a wife and four children. The older brother was not married.

The brothers were poor farmers, working their one small field together.

At the end of every season, the brothers would divide the

harvest equally, and then each brother would gather his sheaves of wheat and stack them outside his house.

One year, after the harvest, the older brother awoke from his sleep and said to himself, "How unfair I have been. My brother and I have been sharing the harvest equally. But he has a wife and four children. I have no one to feed but myself. My brother should have a larger share of our harvest."

So in the middle of the night, the older brother secretly carried a large number of his sheaves of wheat over to his brother's house, and added them to the sheaves already belonging to his brother.

Meanwhile, that same night, the younger brother also awoke from his sleep. He said to himself, "All these years, my brother and I have been dividing our harvest into two equal shares. But how unfair I have been. I have four children who will provide for me in my old age—they will give me and their mother a place to sleep and food to eat. But my brother has no one. When he grows old, there won't be anyone to take care of him. My brother should have a larger share of our harvest."

So in the middle of the night, the younger brother secretly carried a large number of his sheaves of wheat over to his brother's house, and added them to the sheaves already belonging to his brother.

For many nights, each brother took a portion of his sheaves and added it to the other's.

And each morning as the brothers looked at their own sheaves, each one was amazed to find that his sheaves had not grown any smaller in number.

But one night as each brother carried sheaves to the other's house, they came upon each other on the road.

Each brother quickly understood what the other was trying to do, and why his own sheaves had not diminished. They embraced and wept and kissed each other in brotherly love.

According to legend, God saw the brothers embracing and said, "Blessed is the field where these two brothers stand."

Centuries later, when King Solomon built the Holy Temple, it was on the very spot where the brothers had met, for it was holy ground.

Your office, your factory, your showroom, can become a sacred place when you treat everyone you encounter with love and respect.

Your business, your company, your profession, can become a sacred calling when you embrace everyone you meet in kindness and compassion.

Your brothers and sisters are waiting to meet you halfway.

Your work world is ready to be blessed.

Every human being is distinct and unique.

Yet all human beings are interconnected, much like the waves described by the poet Walt Whitman, "rolling over each other and interwetting each other."

You can best achieve and succeed in life—and surely in business—when you recognize the infinite worth of each human being, when you celebrate the shared oneness of all human beings, when you forge a partnership of purpose with every human being.

For in the words of the Indian proverb, "When I know who I am, I am you."

The Fifth Commandment

~

"DO JUSTLY,

LOVE MERCY,

AND WALK

HUMBLY"

Not long ago a young couple came to talk to me about plans for their wedding. They wanted the ceremony to be held in a beautiful park overlooking the Pacific Ocean. But they had one concern.

The woman said to me, "We know that there is usually wonderful sunny weather here in San Diego. But what if it rains on the day of our wedding? The rain will ruin everything."

We talked about calling the weather bureau for a long-range forecast. We tried to determine the odds of it raining on that particular day. We discussed contingency plans and alternate sites in case of rain. And then, after weighing all the pros and cons, the couple decided to go ahead with the original plan—to have their wedding in the park.

As they were leaving, the young man turned to me and said,

"Thank you for your advice and for your help. But now, to make sure that it doesn't rain on the day of our wedding, please have a talk with The Man Upstairs. Pray for sunshine. After all, you're a rabbi. He'll listen to you."

I did not want to get into a long discussion about *my* ability to pray being any better than anyone else's, or even of the value of a prayer for or against rain. So I laughingly said, "I'd like to help, but I'm only in *sales,* not *management.*"

There are some things—like rainfall at a certain time in a certain place—that, try as we will, human beings just cannot control.

Yet so much of life, so much of human interaction—especially in the world of business—calls for taking charge; for competent, effective management; for inspired, visionary leadership.

At one time or another, in one form or another, almost every person who works in the world of business will be called on to manage and to lead. For to paraphrase, "Some are born to leadership, some achieve leadership, and some have leadership thrust upon them."

It takes very special talent, very special skills, very special commitment, to be in management—to be responsible for directing and affecting other people's work and careers.

The tale is told that when the great teacher and sage Yehudi died in the little Eastern European village of Pzhysha in the early 1800s, his disciples did not know whom to choose for their new master. They turned to Rabbi Simcha Bunam to advise them.

Rabbi Bunam said, "A shepherd was tending his sheep close by a beautiful, green meadow, near a sparkling spring. He feared that a wolf might come and snatch away his sheep, so he resolved to keep a most watchful eye. But at nightfall, growing very tired, he lay down on the ground and fell asleep. Near midnight he awoke with a start. He was immediately dismayed and afraid, for never before had he fallen asleep while watching over his flock. He rushed to his sheep, lying in the meadow, and saw them crowded up against each other. He counted them, and none was missing. Then he cried out, 'Dear God, how can I repay you? Entrust your sheep to me once more, and never again will I neglect them. I will guard them with my very life.'"

Rabbi Bunam said, "Find such a shepherd and make him your master."

In the contemporary business world managers are often chosen for their longevity with the company and for their skill at negotiating the climb up the corporate ladder.

Once in place, managers often get caught up in the need to beat the competition and to meet the bottom line. Compelled by the pressure to perform, some managers forget to serve as encouraging guides, becoming, instead, harsh taskmasters.

But to be a real leader means to be a shepherd to a flock, to protect and defend, to nurture growth and tend to needs. To be a leader means to consider each life in your care as precious as your own.

Management—leadership—can be hard, it can be scary, it can be lonely. So many people depend on you. So much rides on each decision. So much is at stake with every call.

How do you do it? How do you rise up to leadership?

How do you balance the needs of your people with your need to produce and profit?

How do you become the manager who is respected for wisdom and judgment, who is appreciated for integrity and fairness, who is admired for understanding and concern?

How do you become the leader you want to be—a teacher, a mentor, a guide?

Ancient wisdom offers advice—a simple yet profound formula to guide everyone who leads, anyone who aspires to leadership: "Do justly, love mercy, and walk humbly."

Warren Bennis, Distinguished Professor of Business Administration at the University of Southern California, recently described as "the poet-philosopher-scholar of business life, a management guru," teaches, "Managers do things right. Leaders do the right thing."

As a manager striving to be a true leader, you can do the right thing when you *do justly,* when you set the right tone and create the right atmosphere in which to do business.

How do your employees know your company's philosophy of doing business? Its sense of identity? Its mission? Its purposes? Its values? Its commitments? How do your employees know how they are to represent your company and what it stands for?

A company "mission statement" may help. Company policies may set the direction. But a company's business ethic is best conveyed when it trickles down from the top, when each and every person—from the CEO to every line manager—lives and reflects the company's commitment to doing justly, to honesty, integrity, and decency.

A manager-leader can be the embodiment of the company's ethic, teaching by model and example.

In his book *Way of the Peaceful Warrior,* Dan Millman tells of the mother who brought her son to Mahatma Gandhi. She said, "Please, Gandhi, please tell my son to stop eating sugar."

Gandhi looked at the young boy for a long time. Then he said to the mother, "Bring your son back to me in two weeks."

The mother did not understand why Gandhi would delay his instruction to her son, but she did as she was asked.

Two weeks later, she and her son returned. Gandhi looked deeply into the boy's eyes and said, "Stop eating sugar."

The mother was grateful, but puzzled. She asked, "Why did you send us away for two weeks? Why didn't you tell my son to stop eating sugar two weeks ago when we were here?"

And Gandhi replied, "Two weeks ago, *I* was eating sugar."

What kind of manager-leader, what kind of role model, will *you* be? What kind of personal example will you set? What work environment will you create? What sense of right and wrong will you establish?

As you make your choices and create your style, remember your power and your influence. For your people will mirror and then adopt your commitments as they see you living them. They will be like the little boy following his father on a climb up a steep mountain who said, "Be careful, Daddy, I'm walking in your footsteps."

When you do justly, you forge the right path for everyone to follow.

And doing justly as a manager-leader means evaluating wisely, choosing courageously, and then standing together with your people to implement the choices you make, the decisions you render.

One kind of manager tells people how to behave and then sits back waiting to see what happens. This manager says, "I've decided what is best for you. Now *you* go ahead and do it."

The other kind of manager says, "My best judgment tells me that this is what we should do. Let's do it together. I'll lead the way. *Follow me!*"

This is a manager who leads with deeds, who is willing to take risks, to accept responsibility. This is a leader who does not yell "Charge!" from the safety of the command post, but leads the troops from the front of the line.

This is the kind of leader that you can be when—for yourself and with your people—you follow the advice of the contemporary actor Alan Alda: "Be bold. When you embark for strange places, don't leave any of yourself safely on the shore. Have the nerve to go into unexplored territory. You have to leave the city of your comfort and go into the wilderness of your intuition. What you discover will be wonderful. What you discover will be yourself."

When you do justly, you lead the way toward self-discovery, opportunity, and growth.

And doing justly as a manager-leader means dealing in good faith, being aboveboard, being open, being fair, being consistent.

It means giving gentle instruction and strong encouragement.
It means offering assistance, support, and advice.
It means listening and understanding.
It means appreciating each individual and nurturing potential.
It means being a motivator, a cheerleader, an ego booster.
It means fostering self-esteem and enabling empowerment.

I have never understood some of my colleagues at the university who boast, "I never give an A," or the registrar who keeps sending out memos warning about "grade inflation," and cautioning professors about giving out too many A's and B's.

I would consider my semester to be a blazing success if *every* student earned an A!

For if every student learns all that I set out to teach, and demonstrates—through objective standards—that the material is mastered, then the goal of the educational process, the goal of my classroom, is met. I have taught well and my students have learned well.

Who could ask for a better performance review—as a learner or as a teacher—than when everyone does the best possible work, when all the goals are met, when everyone succeeds?

It is exactly the same for workers and managers.

You can be a most successful manager, a powerful, influential leader, when you teach your people all that you have to teach, when you inspire your people to meet their goals, when your people perform the best they can, when you and your people achieve the very most for your company.

When you do justly, you give your people victories.

As a manager, striving to be a true leader, you can increase your effectiveness, you can add to your success, when, as well as doing justly, you *love mercy.*

When your people need guidance and direction, you can be patient and gracious. When your people need support and encouragement, you can be kind and generous. When your people are confused or uncertain, you can be compassionate and consoling. When your people make mistakes—as surely they will—you can be understanding and forgiving. When your people achieve success, you can be complimentary and proud.

You love mercy when you understand where your people are "coming from," and when you wisely and gently help them rise up to where you want them to be.

There was once a king who had a son, a prince, who thought that he was a rooster. The prince took off all his clothes, sat under the table, and ate corn.

The king offered a great reward to anyone who could convince the prince that he was not a rooster. Wise man after sage tried and tried, but no one could convince the prince that he was not a rooster.

Then one simple man came along and took off all his clothes. He sat under the table with the prince-rooster and ate corn. He said to the prince, "Cock-a-doodle-do."

The prince asked, "Hey, are you a rooster?" And the man answered, "Of course I am a rooster." The prince was very pleased to have a companion rooster. And the two of them happily munched corn under the table.

Soon the man got up and put on his clothes. The prince said, "Roosters don't wear clothes." And the man said, "I am cold. Would it make me any less of a rooster if I wear pants and a shirt?" And the prince said, "No, I guess not."

A little later, the man got up from the ground and sat at the table. The prince said, "Roosters don't sit at tables." The man replied, "I am very tired, and the ground is very hard. Would it make me any less of a rooster if I sat at the table?" And the prince said, "No, I guess not."

And soon the man began eating regular food. The prince said, "Roosters don't eat regular food. We only eat corn." And the man said, "I am very hungry, and I am very tired of corn. Would it make me any less of a rooster if I ate regular food?" And the prince said, "No, I guess not."

And not long after that, the prince was sitting at the table, wearing clothes and eating regular food, right along with his friend the other rooster.

You can best lead when you truly understand your people, when you respond to their needs, feel their pain, and share their joy.

You can lead best when you do not remain above the fray, when you don't stand isolated and insulated, but when you are willing to get your hands dirty, to do whatever it takes to help your people reach their goals.

A master taught, "If you want to raise a man from mud [in our case, from bewilderment, failure, struggle, or difficulty] do not think that it is enough to keep standing on top and reaching down to give him a helping hand. You must go down all the way yourself, down into the mud. Then take hold of him with strong hands and pull him and yourself into the light."

Yet try as you might, inevitably there will be confrontations with colleagues, crises with customers, disputes with competitors. There will be disagreements and heated discussions. There will be office politics, and unfortunately, there will be a showdown now and then. There will be disillusionment, offended sensibilities, and hurt feelings. There will be tension and occasional ill will.

You love mercy when you understand that your most important task as a manager-leader is to love peace and pursue peace.

Every night, when a certain man came home from work, his little boy would run and jump up into his arms and ask, "Daddy, will you play with me? Will you, Daddy, will you?" And, almost every night, this man played with his son, sharing games and books and toys and talk.

But one night the father was very tired. So instead of rushing to play with his son, he sat down in his chair, opened his newspaper and began to read. As on every other night, his son asked, "Daddy, will you play with me?" But on this night the father replied, "Oh, not tonight. I'm just too tired." The little boy kept asking, but the father's reply did not change.

Finally, to keep his son occupied—and frankly, to get a little peace and quiet—the father took a whole page out of his newspaper. Printed on the page was a map of the world. He took a scissors and cut the map into many small pieces and said to his son, "Here is a puzzle of a map of the world. Why don't you go into your room and put the puzzle together."

The father thought that his son would be gone for a long time, but the boy was back in just a few minutes. The father was amazed. He said, "How did you finish the puzzle so quickly? The map of the world is so large and complicated. How did you put it together so soon?"

And the little boy replied, "It was easy. You see, on the back of the picture of the world was a picture of a man. I just put the man together and the world fell right into place."

The whole world of your business will fall right into place when you love mercy by loving peace—by celebrating the dignity and the worth of each and every human being you manage and lead.

Sensitive human feelings and the world in which you do business are counting on you, for "Blessed is the peacemaker."

You can be the healer, you can be the reconciler, you can be the peacemaker.

As a manager striving to be a true leader, you accomplish the most when you *walk humbly*, when you are modest and unpretentious, when you leave pride and arrogance and power trips at the front door.

A man who pursued honors came to Rabbi Bunam—the same Rabbi Bunam of the story of the shepherd—and said, "My father has appeared to me in a dream and told me that I am to be a leader of men."

Rabbi Bunam listened to the story in silence.

Soon afterward the same man returned to the rabbi and said, "I have had the same dream night after night. My father appears to me to announce that I am destined to be a leader of men."

"I understand," said the rabbi, "that you are ready to become a leader of men. Now if your father comes to you in a dream once more, tell him that you are prepared to become a leader of men, but that he should now also appear to the people you are supposed to lead to tell them."

No memo from headquarters, no unilateral declaration, no interdepartmental power struggle, no office coup, ever created a true leader.

You can never become a true leader by foisting yourself on others, by flaunting power, by demanding loyalty.

Rather, you can rise to leadership through quiet determination, gentle persuasion, humble presence.

You can become a true leader when you *earn* the respect, the allegiance, and the admiration of those you seek to guide.

You can become a true leader when you truly understand that your power comes not from those who appoint you, not from your own sense of self-importance, but from the permission, acceptance, and grace of those you lead.

You can become a true leader when you understand the wisdom of the ancient sage who said, "I have learned much from my teachers, even more from my colleagues, but from my students, I have learned the most."

One day a recently appointed vice president was called into the office of the chairman of the board.

The chairman said, "I have some troubling news to tell you. Your people have been complaining about you. They say that you are aloof and unreachable; they say that you do not listen to their ideas; they say that you do not make time to work with them and help them. They say that you just sit in your office, talk on your telephone, and go out for long lunches with your friends."

The vice president was stunned by the accusations and began to protest his innocence.

So the chairman of the board took the vice president over to the window and said, "Look out there. What do you see?"

The vice president looked and replied, "I see people out on the street."

Then, the chairman took the vice president over to a mirror hanging on the wall. "What do you see now?" he asked.

The vice president looked into the mirror and said, "Now I see myself."

"Ah," said the chairman. "In the window there is glass, and in the mirror there is glass. But the glass of the mirror is covered with a little silver. No sooner has the silver been added— no sooner do you have position and power, some fame and some fortune—then you cease to see others, but see only yourself."

When you walk humbly, you understand that the very best leader is, in reality, the very best servant.

And you can be the best manager, the best leader, when you serve selflessly and with a full heart, when you care for and cherish your people, when you meet their needs as if they were your very own.

One of the greatest leaders who ever lived was Moses.

Following the dictates of God, Moses confronted Pharaoh, brought the ten plagues upon Egypt, freed his people from bondage, and led them across the Red Sea. He stood with them in battle against foes who tried to destroy them. He climbed to the top of the mountain to receive the Law. He guided his people on the long journey in the wilderness.

Through it all he patiently listened to the cries of the people when they complained about lack of food, lack of water, lack of comfort.

One day the people cried out more bitterly than ever before. They were thirsty, so thirsty, and there was no water. They came to Moses. "Find us water," they cried, "lest we die here in the desert."

Moses turned to God. "What shall I do?" he asked. "Where will I find water for these thirsty people?"

And God said, "Speak to that rock over there, and it will bring forth water."

But Moses did not speak to the rock. Instead he hit it with his staff. Water gushed forth, and the people drank and were satisfied.

But God was very angry. He said to Moses, "I told you to speak to the rock, but instead you hit it. You must be punished. Moses, you will not be able to enter into the Promised Land."

Not enter the Promised Land? Just for hitting the rock? After all he did for his God and his people, Moses is to be denied the prize, the payoff, the reward for all his labors?

It seems grossly unfair.

But the real problem was not that Moses had hit the rock, or even that he had disobeyed God's instructions.

What happened was that Moses was exhausted, "burned out," angry, from the people's constant complaints and never-ending demands. Rather than being able to speak to the rock—as he knew he should do, and as he knew would bring result—he struck out at it in frustration and fury.

Moses could not lead the people into the Promised Land, not because he had hit the rock but because he no longer possessed the qualities of leadership. He had forgotten to do justly, love mercy, and walk humbly.

You are a Moses. For you—like every person—want to enter the promised land of your own desires in your own lifetime.

Like Moses, you can be denied the ultimate prize of satisfaction and fulfillment in your work if you forget what it takes to be a real leader.

Or you can lead the way into the promised land of accomplishment and success—bringing with you all the people with whom you work—if only you will remember the words of David Wolpe, in his book *The Healer of Shattered Hearts:* "For each of us, the question is not how we slay the dragon, but how we tend the sheep."

The promised land awaits you. The sheep await their shepherd.

The Sixth Commandment

~

"BRING HEALING

AND CURE"

It must be wonderful to be a survey-taking pollster.

How happy it must make people to be approached by a person—clipboard in hand, pencil poised—to be asked, "What do you think? What is your opinion? What is your choice? What do you feel?"

How happy it must make people to know that someone will really listen.

How happy it must make people to assume that someone really cares.

How happy it must make people to sense that they are really important, and what they think and feel really, really counts.

How many thousands of times have you said, "Hi. How are you?"

How often have you expected—or even wanted—a truthful answer?

How much do you really know about the feelings, the welfare, the health, the well-being of those with whom you work?

Yet ultimately what is more important than the physical and mental health of those who work with and for you?

Your people's own personal well-being and peace of mind—and their productivity at work—so very often depend on how safe, how secure, how protected they feel.

For very few people can leave all feelings, all emotions, all concerns—sorrows *or* joys—at the office door. Every day there are those who come to work with personal issues swirling within: illness, physical pain, marital strife, a sick child, a dying parent, a newfound love, a daughter's graduation, a son's wedding.

What role or responsibility does your company, your business, have in providing for the safety and protection, the health and dignity, of your people?

Across the distance of more than three thousand years, the Bible offers direction:

> If two men fight, and one hits the other with a stone or with his fist, and the injured one does not die, but has to stay in bed because of his injuries, if he is able to rise again and walk around, then the one who hurt him shall not be judged guilty. But, he must pay for the loss of the injured one's time, and pay him to be thoroughly healed.

Isn't that incredible!

More than three millennia ago, the Bible required the payment of medical bills and compensation for lost wages for one who was injured by another.

In modern terms this means that you can inspire confidence in your workplace by making sure that the work space and the working conditions are safe and secure. And if injury occurs, you can provide the time and the money to insure complete healing.

It means that you can assure that all of your people—and their families—are adequately protected, by providing comprehensive medical, dental, disability, and life insurances.

Not only will your people benefit, but you and your business will gain, for an employee who feels appreciated and well cared for will be a better, a more effective, a more productive employee. A worker who knows that his or her family is protected in case of trauma or tragedy will be a more content, a more loyal worker.

Yet there is so much more that you can do besides providing care in illness or injury.

You can help prevent pain and suffering before they happen.

Preventive health care can include providing for a comprehensive annual physical examination, for gyms and running tracks and workout equipment in the workplace, for stress-reduction clinics, and for in-house psychologists or social workers to offer counsel and advice. Preventive health care can even mean a roving massage therapist to give ten-minute "at-your-desk" neck-and-shoulder massages to relax and re-invigorate.

With preventive health care, more and more serious and long-lasting illnesses can be averted, which can mean healthier, more productive workers.

And for the company or business, it can mean less absenteeism, fewer paid sick days, and fewer lost hours of production and productivity.

With preventive health care, everybody wins.

Yet helping to promote physical health is only half the need.

The last few years have begun to bring growing realization that *two* pieces of ancient wisdom both have significant modern relevance.

Buddha taught: "To keep the body in good health is a

duty...otherwise we shall not be able to keep our minds strong and clear."

A healthy body helps create a healthy mind.

And the Bible teaches, "As a person thinks, so he is."

A healthy mind helps create a healthy body.

Modern visionaries such as Norman Cousins, Dr. Bernie Siegel, and Dr. Deepak Chopra teach of the inextricable connection between mind and body—what is being called "holistic health."

A pain-racked body can often keep the mind from creativity and transcendence. Negative thoughts and pessimistic projections can often cause the body harm or keep it from healing.

What you think and what you feel can mean illness or health, continuing sickness or rapid recovery.

As Norman Cousins explains it, "The greatest force in the human body is the natural drive of the body to heal itself—but that force is not independent of the belief system, which can translate expectations into psychological change. Nothing is more wondrous about the fifteen billion neurons in the human brain than their ability to convert thoughts, hopes, ideas, and attitudes into chemical substances (which can cure the ailing body). Everything, therefore, begins with belief."

You can help your people be healthy and well when you hear their concerns, and also their unspoken words, when you share their joy, feel their pain, celebrate their triumphs, and comfort them in their sorrow.

You can help your people do their best work when you see not just the worker—and the role he or she plays in your plans—but the person—a whole human being—who feels and responds, who laughs and cries, who hurts and can heal.

You do the most for your business when you have healthy, happy people. And you have healthy, happy people when you take care of them and meet their needs.

Do you remember the story of the princess and the pea?

No matter how many soft, fluffy mattresses were piled high for the princess to sleep on, she still could feel the one tiny little pea underneath the very first mattress.

Only when that pea was removed could she sleep comfortably and peacefully.

It is not just catastrophic illness or traumatic injury or deep tragedy that keeps a worker from focusing, from concentrating, from doing good work. It is, as well—and sometimes more so—the little nagging irritants of personal hurts and anxieties—the one little pea under the mattress—that prevent comfort of body and peace of mind.

You can help remove the obstacles that keep your people from doing their best when your company or business provides ways to promote both personal health and emotional serenity, ways to help alleviate the personal worries and concerns that trouble your people.

Many companies are replacing the fat- and cholesterol-laden meals in the company cafeteria with more fruits and vegetables and grains, more salt-free and fat-free menus. The "three-martini lunch" has given way not just to dwindling expense accounts but to the realization that a healthy worker is a better worker.

Many companies are putting fine art on the walls and magnificent sculptures on the grounds, and are playing sweet music through public speakers or private headphones, knowing that the environment in which people work affects performance, knowing that being surrounded by artistic and musical beauty soothes the soul, bringing both quiet calm and creative inspiration, motivating workers to do their best.

Many companies are responding to the very real problems of substance abuse by providing drug and alcohol counseling, rehabilitation programs and stays in rehabilitation centers.

Feeling a sense of responsibility for the recovery of each and every person, these companies are helping to turn tragedy into hope.

Many companies are extending maternity leave for longer periods, knowing that mothers need significant time to bond with their newborn babies. And some companies are providing for paternity leave as well, recognizing that a baby has a father who needs to bond with his child, too.

Many companies are creating in-house day-care centers and after-school programs for the children of their people, providing a safe and secure environment for the children, and reassurance and peace of mind for the parent-workers.

Many companies are creating flextime working schedules so that parents can be with their children in the hours that they are most needed, all the while doing the work that the job requires.

Many companies—with or without government mandate—are now arranging for family leave for workers who need to care for a seriously ill child or a parent, recognizing that family ties and the sense of family responsibility are vital components of human existence.

Many companies are offering extended grief leave after the death of a loved one, recognizing that it cannot be "business as usual" for a worker whose parent, spouse, or child has just died.

Some companies are sponsoring summer camp programs for the children of their people, knowing that there are better places to play and grow than the hot summer city streets, and easing the fears of the parent-workers who worry about their children during those long, idle hours.

Some companies are providing their people with the use of a retreat center for family holidays and vacations, knowing that busy workers need time to reconnect with their spouses and children in a tranquil, inexpensive, fun-filled setting.

Some companies are offering college scholarships to the children of their people, knowing that college costs are a heavy financial burden, and knowing that the best investment in tomorrow is the investment in young people today.

Some companies make sure that a worker who marks an important life occasion—marriage, the birth of a child, a child's First Holy Communion, a child's Bar or Bas Mitzvah, a child's college graduation, a child's wedding, a milestone anniversary or birthday, the birth of a grandchild—or who is bereaved by the death of a loved one, receives a personal phone call, a handwritten note, or even a personal visit from a prominent representative of the company. This kind of personal recognition and expression of sentiment is much appreciated and long remembered, for it is tangible evidence of the company's commitment to the lives and the feelings of its people.

Some companies are demonstrating deep sensitivity when long-tenured and excellent employees are laid off and terminated—which is occurring more and more often in these tough economic times. In addition to compassionate "exit interviews" and the offer of office space and secretarial assistance to help in a new job search, a few companies have begun placing ads in local and national newspapers announcing the availability of their people. One recent ad said:

> Experienced Employees Available. Resulting from the closing of our local Distribution Center, employees of our company experienced in accounting, customer service, computer operations, secretarial, inventory control, telemarketing and distribution management will be available. To arrange for an interview, please call...

The bitterness and fear of job loss is tempered by the company's openhearted assistance and sincere concern for the feelings and the future of each and every one of its people.

A company's commitment to the physical and emotional health and well-being of its people and their families is not just an idealistic dream. Companies across America are beginning to learn that taking good care of their people means both increased worker satisfaction *and* increased productivity and profit.

When President Clinton signed the Family Leave Bill into law, the chief executive officers and two randomly selected employees from Fel-Pro, in Skokie, Illinois, were invited to the White House to witness the signing, for Fel-Pro has had a model family leave policy in place for more than ten years.

For decades, Fel-Pro has had a whole menu of employee benefits that include family and maternity leave, on-site day care, summer camps, school tutoring and college scholarships for the children of employees, elder care, psychological and legal counseling, and more.

Recently, *New Woman* magazine noted that nightshift workers at Fel-Pro can take a sixteen-week course on parenting skills, offered at 3:45 A.M.

Fel-Pro has found that spending the time and the money it takes to treat its people with dignity and respect has more than paid off, for the company has enjoyed more than fifty straight years of profitability.

Says Fel-Pro chairman emeritus Lewis Weinberg, "As in marriage, you get out of any relationship what you put into it. You've got to invest in order to receive. We find by our experience that in so doing, we can be successful and profitable."

Companies that sponsor these kinds of programs are deserving of admiration and praise—and imitation—for their commitment to their people. Yet no company can be a Santa Claus, expending unlimited amounts of money and time in employee benefits.

Thus every worker—and no matter what position you hold

or how much responsibility you have, unless you own your own business, you are a worker—can enhance the company's desire and ability to help its people. When you monitor yourself and use only what you really need, when you play fair and don't take advantage of what is offered, you join in containing costs and keeping benefits available.

In the words of an old axiom, "If I am not for myself, who will be for me? But if I am only for myself, what am I?"

Long, long ago—so the fable goes—a slave named Androcles escaped from his cruel master. He fled into the forest on the outskirts of his town.

As he walked deep into the woods, he heard the great roar of an animal crying out in pain.

He followed the sound into a small clearing, where he saw a huge, sleek lion, with a deep golden coat and a magnificent mane, bellowing in agony and licking its paw.

He said, "O great lion, what is wrong?"

The lion said, "I have this sharp thorn deeply embedded in my paw. I can't get it out, and it hurts very, very much."

Androcles approached the lion and said, "Here, let me see if I can help you." He took the lion's paw in his own hand, and with a small knife he took from his pocket, he worked the thorn out of the lion's paw.

"Oh, thank you, sir," said the lion. "Thank you very much."

"I'm glad that I was able to help," said Androcles.

And from that day on, the lion and the man were constant companions.

One day, when Androcles and the lion were out for a walk, they were captured and taken to the city to be displayed by the circus.

The plan was simple: The lion would be denied food for many days—making him very hungry and very ferocious.

Then the man would be fed to the lion, and the bloodthirsty crowd could watch the man being devoured.

On the appointed day the emperor and all the court came to see the spectacle.

Androcles was led into the amphitheater. The roar of the crowd filled him with fear, and sadness filled his heart, for this was to be the end of him.

From the opposite side of the amphitheater, a door was opened, and the lion was let loose.

The hungry lion rushed toward its victim, stood up on its hind legs, opened its mouth wide, and was about to eat the man in one big gulp.

But at the very last second, the lion looked carefully at its prey and recognized its friend. Instead of biting off the man's head, the lion draped its paws around the man's shoulders and began to gently lick his face.

The roaring crowd became utterly silent. The emperor was so astonished by what he had seen that he decided that the man must have special magical powers. Immediately he set the man free, and ordered that the lion be returned to the forest.

And so, rather than meet his death, Androcles left the amphitheater alive and well, saved by his old friend—the lion, from whose paw he had once removed a thorn.

When you take care of your people, they will take care of you—and your business.

Yet even with the need to be intimately involved in the lives of people with whom you work, there is an important and serious caution. For there is a clear line of distinction, a delicate balance, between professional concern and personal interference.

What is the difference between caring and meddling? Between sincere intent and ulterior motive? Between a compliment and a "come-on"?

Seemingly the line of distinction is being crossed and the delicate balance has been upset, for in recent days charges of sexual harassment have filled the business world—accusations ranging from untoward comments, licentious looks, and unwanted touches to solicitation of sex, demands for ongoing sexual liaisons, and rape.

Some of the accused admit to using the old "casting-couch" technique, expecting sexual favors in return for career advancement. Some admit that seeking sex—or speaking with sexual overtones or innuendo—in the workplace has far less to do with sex than with the powerful taking advantage of the powerless.

But some are genuinely confused. Jokes, banter, and comments that once seemed playful and harmless are now considered inappropriate and improper.

So how do you walk that fine line, how do you keep that delicate balance, between sincere concern for the lives of your people and not violating their personal feelings, sensibilities, or boundaries?

Here is a basic rule. It may seem simplistic, but it works. If you follow it, issues of sexual harassment can begin to be eliminated from the workplace.

The rule is: "If you wouldn't say it or do it to your mother or your sister, don't say it or do it to your coworker."

And because sexual harassment is not limited to men, women can follow this basic rule: "If you wouldn't say it or do it to your father or your brother, don't say it or do it to your coworker."

With personal behavior modified, men and women working together in business can then begin to take the steps that will help eliminate not only individual sexual harassment in the workplace, but the atmosphere in society that sanctions—and even celebrates—using sex as a means to achieving goals and attaining desires.

For some of the very people who rightly complain about sexual harassment are the very same people who sit in marketing agencies and corporate boardrooms creating advertising campaigns that use scantily clothed women and mostly naked men, sexually charged language, and the lure of sexual conquest to sell automobiles, blue jeans, beer, and almost everything else.

If you want to help end sexual harassment and innuendo in your own workplace, then you can best start by helping to eliminate the use of "sex-to-sell" in the marketplace.

You can help create a new business environment where sex is neither used nor abused, where people are neither used nor abused, where products and services are sold on their own merit, where every person is treated with dignity and respect.

From your awareness of the mistrust and pain that sexual harassment can cause in the marketplace, and with your commitment to rid the work world of unnecessary and undesirable sexual overtones, you can help bring new balance, renewed safety, and deep healing to the workplace.

As Ralph Waldo Emerson taught, "The wounded oyster mends its shell with pearl."

Even the very best health care and the deepest concern for your people is not enough to bring full healing and cure, for people do not exist alone.

We are all an intricate, interconnected part of the universe in which we live. And the health of the universe determines the health of each human being.

In the words of Native American leader Chief Seattle, "This we know. The earth does not belong to man; man belongs to the earth. This we know. All things are connected, like the blood that unites one family. All things are connected. Whatever befalls the earth, befalls the sons of earth. Man does not weave the web of life, he is merely a strand in it. Whatever he does to the web, he does to himself."

"The earth is the Lord's"—but it has been given to *us* to share, to admire, to enjoy: the fluffy clouds in the rich, blue sky; the fiery sun sinking into the wide horizon; the big yellow moon and the twinkling stars; the rolling waves of the ocean and the gentle flow of the rivers; the tall, stately trees and the green, green grass; the mooing cows, the chirping birds, the bleating sheep, the roaring lions, the buzzing bees, and the delicate, fluttering butterflies.

What a great gift we have been given!

But oh, how we have despoiled it!

We have choked the sky with the smog of our factory chimneys and our automobile emissions.

We have polluted the rivers and streams with our industrial toxic waste.

We have cut down whole forests just to print the Sunday newspaper, and we have destroyed the trees to make paper towels, wooden toothpicks, and cardboard boxes—all used once and thrown away.

We have raped the land of her sparkling minerals to bejewel our fingers, and we have stripped the land of her resources to fuel our never-ending consumption.

We have depleted the ozone layer with our aerosol spray cans, laying the rain forests bare and causing global warming.

And we have disposed of our garbage thoughtlessly and recklessly, so that our mountains of aluminum cans and plastic bottles will still be standing tall on the road to eternity.

And the earth is crying out to us in her pain.

To begin to safeguard the environment, to preserve the earth, to protect the planet, to save the universe, your business, your company, can begin to heal instead of harm.

You can make sure that your smokestacks do not pollute and your chemicals do not poison. You can make certain that you respect resources, save water, recycle, and replace.

If you contaminate a river, you can clean up a river.

If you befoul the air, you can purify the air.

If you cut down a tree—or use a forest of paper in your copying machine—you can plant a tree.

You can search for new fuels that will do less harm. You can develop new methods to renew resources. You can find new technologies that can restore and sustain the place in which we all live.

Convenience, expediency, higher profits, all pale in importance when you realize that what is at stake here is the air you—and your children—breathe, the water you drink, and the protection you have from the ultraviolet rays of the sun.

What is at stake here is not just the quality of life, but *life itself.*

So when you and your business decide to take positive, proactive steps to help heal and save the universe, you are really saving yourself.

As the contemporary spiritual guide Ram Dass explains, "In the ultimate depth of being, we find ourselves no longer separate, but, rather, part of the unity of the universe. That unity includes the sufferer and the suffering, and the healer and that which heals. Therefore, all acts of healing are ultimately ourselves healing our Self."

Your commitment to heal the earth may, at the outset, seem self-defeating—for your competitors may not join you, and your profits may suffer.

But consumers are more and more aware of the needs of the earth, and are becoming more and more determined to use products from companies committed to protecting and preserving both natural resources and the environment.

That is why, in recent years, consumers have prevailed upon companies to reformulate ingredients, restructure manufacturing, change packaging, use recycled paper and plastics, and institute a host of other changes—all sensitive to environmental concerns.

When your business practices profit the universe, your business will, in turn, earn profit for you.

And your commitment to heal the earth may, at the outset, seem overwhelming—for there is so much to do, so much that must be preserved.

Surely you cannot do it all at once, and perhaps you may not see results—not even in your lifetime.

But you can begin.

A sage once passed through a field where he saw an old man planting an oak tree.

"Why are you planting that tree?" he asked. "Surely you do not expect to live long enough to see the acorn grow into an oak?"

The old man replied, "I will not live that long, but I must plant this tree. When I came into this world, I could enjoy the shade and the fruit of the trees my ancestors had planted for me. I am planting now so that my children's children will have trees when they come into this world."

Existence as it is and as it will be—the fate and the future of our planet—is yours to determine.

Will you bring protection and healing?

Will you safeguard the great trust that you have been given?

The great Native American leader Sitting Bull offered the challenge: "Let us put our minds together and see what we shall make for our children."

There once was a traveler on a long, long journey. He had walked for miles and miles, and he was hot and tired, hungry and thirsty.

Finally he came to a large, leafy tree.

He sat against its strong trunk to rest. He was cooled by the shade of its leaves. He ate of its fruit and drank of its sweet juices.

When he was ready to continue on his journey, the traveler said to the tree, "How may I thank you, how may I bless you, for all you have given me? I would like to bless you with abundance, but you already have everything: You have a strong trunk to give comfort; you have wide leaves to bring refreshment; you have delicious, juicy fruit to quench thirst and satisfy hunger. You already have everything. How may I bless you?"

"There is but one blessing I can give, and this is how I bless you: 'May your seeds be like you.'"

May your seeds be like you.

May your children, and your children's children, and generations yet unborn rejoice in the earth—the earth protected, healed, and preserved by you.

A sage taught, "There is no wealth like health."

And your grandmother probably said, "Everything will be all right—as long as you have your health."

One of America's most successful entrepreneurs and wealthiest men watched helplessly as his teenage son slowly died of brain cancer.

He gladly would have traded all that he is, all that he has, all that he will ever become, for the life of his child.

He—and we—know: Fame and fortune are fleeting and insignificant.

There is nothing more important than good health.

Surely the ultimate decisions about illness or health, life or death, are not in our hands.

But the health of your people, the health of your business, the health of your universe, depend—in great part—on the choices and the commitments you decide to make.

When you wrap your people and your planet in your compassionate care and your holy healing, you can help bring peace to troubled souls, and hope to a battered world.

The Seventh Commandment

~

"YOU SHALL

SURELY TITHE"

Long before there were annual reports, long before there were profit-and-loss statements, long before there were pretax earnings and tax deductions for charitable contributions, there was the basic human instinct to care for each other.

That is why, long ago, we were all told, "You shall surely tithe." From what you earn, give 10 percent to those in need.

From what you receive, you are asked to give.

In modern terms that means from every dollar you make, give a dime to a person or to a cause that needs your help.

You are asked to share your bounty to help feed the hungry and shelter the homeless; to help protect the widow and safeguard the orphan; to uplift the downtrodden and give hope to the brokenhearted.

You can choose any charity, support any cause, respond to any need, but give, you must.

A prince was once lost in a forest for many hours.

Finally he came upon an inn, where he was immediately recognized. He ordered a light meal of fried eggs.

When he finished, the prince asked, "How much do I owe you?"

The innkeeper replied, "Twenty-five rubles."

"Why such an exorbitant price?" asked the prince. "Is there a shortage of eggs in this area?"

"No, there is no shortage of eggs," the innkeeper replied. "We have plenty of eggs. But there is a shortage of princes."

In this country—in this world—where so many need so much, there are not that many who have the means to give.

But you and your company do.

You have the resources to be one of the princes, to share what you have received with those who need.

Giving can be as simple as responding to what is right before your eyes.

An old storyteller relates: "To my grandfather, giving was as simple as taking a walk.

"Once, he came home without his overcoat.

" 'Where's your coat?' my grandmother asked.

" 'Coat? What coat?'

" 'The coat you wore when you left the house.'

" 'Oh, that. I gave it away.'

" 'To whom?' my grandmother asked. 'To whom?'

" 'To a man,' my grandfather said, 'who didn't have a coat.' "

In the world of business, giving is usually more formalized, but it serves the same purpose. Giving provides for those who need.

Most companies encourage their people to help support the local campaign of United Way, the umbrella organization that funds scores of worthy projects and institutions throughout the local community.

Many companies support health research and health care organizations, providing funds to help find the cures for the diseases that ravage us.

Many companies support civic and cultural institutions such as the symphony, the theater, the opera, dance troupes, and museums.

Many companies support educational institutions and programs.

Many companies support direct-service groups that work personally with people in need.

Many companies provide "matching funds," effectively doubling the contributions that their people personally make to favorite causes.

When you and your company give of your monetary resources, you respond to the public interest, the public good.

You are sharing, contributing members of the community and the society in which you live and work—and which supports your business by buying your product.

There is, however, one caution about corporate giving. Consumers—and stockholders of publicly owned companies—have a right to know where corporate funds are going.

While most contributions are given to causes and organizations that enjoy wide public support, some companies choose to give financial gifts to causes that may be considered—by some—to be controversial.

For example, Tom Monaghan, the owner of Domino's Pizza, heavily contributes both company and personal funds to pro-life, antiabortion groups.

Laura Scher and Peter Barnes, owners of Working Assets, a long-distance telephone-carrier company in San Francisco, contribute 1 percent of gross revenues to civil rights, abortion rights, and environmental groups, and provide free long-distance phone calls for customers to lobby politicians and government bureaucrats.

Both these companies—and the many others like them that contribute company funds to special-interest political causes—have every right to "put their money where their mouth is," to financially support their political passions.

But these companies also owe it to their consumers to disclose where contributions are being given.

Then consumers will be fully informed and can choose whether or not to buy a pizza from a company that supports antiabortion groups, and whether or not to make long-distance calls with a company that supports abortion-rights groups.

If your company gives to groups that may be considered controversial, you can make sure that you make public announcements about who receives your gifts.

If you are a consumer—and all of us are—you can ask to be told how the companies you patronize distribute their charitable contributions.

There is no judgment to be made here, for there are good men and women on almost every side of every contemporary social and political issue.

But there is awareness—which companies owe to consumers. And there is choice—which consumers owe it to themselves to make.

Equally important as giving your company funds is giving the work of your company's hands.

Mother Teresa teaches: "There is hunger for ordinary bread, and there is hunger for love, for kindness, for thoughtfulness; and this is the great poverty that makes people suffer so much."

When you open up your heart to give of your time, your care, and your concern, when you give the gift of the work of your hands to those who need you, you give the greatest gift of all—the gift of yourself.

Many companies encourage their people to volunteer time to the myriad people and causes that need more than a check.

Many companies even grant paid time off from the job for a certain number of hours dedicated to volunteer work.

You and your people can offer your time, your energy, your commitment to doing good for the many people who need you: people who are hungry; families without a place to live; children who want to learn to read; teenagers who desperately need direction and guidance; elderly folks who are alone and lonely; the ill, the infirm, the homebound; people who need a chance, a friend, a ray of hope.

Programs like Meals-on-Wheels, which brings food to the homes of the elderly homebound, need not only money to buy food but volunteer drivers to deliver the meals.

Programs like Big Brothers and Big Sisters, which match up fatherless or motherless children with adult friends and role models, need not only money but volunteer adults to be the big brothers and sisters.

Programs like Child-Life, conducted in many children's hospitals, need not only money but volunteers to bring a teddy bear, play a game, help celebrate a holiday, or just talk with a child who is ill.

When you and the people of your company give not only of your financial resources but of your time and your personal efforts, you can come to truly appreciate the real value of your gifts.

For you see the faces and touch the hearts of the people you serve.

Not long ago I was downtown in the city where I live. I was

WAYNE DOSICK

walking from the parking garage where I had left my car to an office building a few blocks away.

As I walked, I noticed many street people sitting in the entryways of buildings, and lounging on bus benches and on the sidewalk. These are the hungry and the homeless of my city, people with few places to go and few opportunities to pursue.

As I walked, I took a few coins from my pocket and gave them to the people I saw.

There is, I know, great debate about the reasons that hunger and homelessness exist in our society. And there is greater debate about how to solve the problem—about whether we should "give a person a fish and feed him for a day, or teach a person to fish and feed him for a lifetime." But at that moment the immediate plight of the starving was more important to me than debates over long-term, permanent solutions. So I took a few coins from my pocket to give to hungry people.

But then something very strange happened.

I began to recognize a few faces.

Who are these people? Do I know them? Are they friends or acquaintances who are down on their luck and have wound up on the streets without my knowing it? These people look *so* familiar. Who are they? What are their names?

And then I realized that a few weeks before, I had volunteered to help serve meals to the hungry at one of my city's food kitchens and shelters. I had spent a Sunday morning serving food to those who came to eat.

And now, as I walked on the city streets, I recognized the faces of the people who had come through the food line. They were no longer just part of a nameless, faceless group that had come for a meal that Sunday morning.

They were individual human beings, who were still hungry on Tuesday afternoon.

When I saw those people, I remembered a lesson that my then-young son taught me many years ago.

For a long time, my family has been putting into modern practice the ancient teaching of Rabbi Tanchum: "Though he needed only one portion of meat for himself, he would buy two; one bunch of vegetables, he would buy two—one for himself and one for the poor."

Every time we go to the supermarket, we buy one extra item—a can of tuna fish, a package of macaroni and cheese, a box of cereal.

We keep these extra items in a bag in the trunk of the car, and when we collect a bagful of groceries, we deliver it to one of the local food pantries that distribute food to the hungry in our city.

One day in the market I took a box of Cheerios from the shelf and said, "This will be our food gift for today."

My son—who was about five or six years old at the time—picked up the box from the shopping cart, put it back on the shelf, and said, "No it won't."

I was rather amazed. I asked, "Why not? Why shouldn't the Cheerios be our food gift for today?"

Reaching for a different box of cereal from the shelf, my son said, "Today we are getting Sugar Frosted Flakes, because there are hungry kids out there, too. And kids like Sugar Frosted Flakes better than Cheerios."

What a great lesson my young son taught me, for he—in his youthful wisdom—had truly seen the faces of the people we were helping to feed.

Even if you don't have a lot of money to give, even if your business is feeling the pinch of tough economic times, you can still respond to the very real needs of very real people by giving the service of your corporate heart and hands.

As Albert Schweitzer put it, "I don't know what your destiny will be, but one thing I do know: the only ones among you who will be really happy are those who have sought and found how to serve."

With your service you can do so much good, you can make such a difference.

The story is told of a righteous woman who was permitted a glimpse of the world to come.

In a lavish palace she was brought into a large room, where she saw hundreds of people sitting at a gigantic banquet table. On the table was a vast array of the most delectable and delicious foods. But not a morsel of food had been touched.

The righteous woman couldn't understand. She asked her guide, "Why aren't these people eating? They look very hungry, and the food looks very good. So why aren't they eating?"

The guide said, "They cannot feed themselves. If you will notice, you will see that each person has his arms bound with rigid splints. He can hold his arms straight out, but he cannot bend them. No matter how hard he tries, he cannot bend his arm to bring his hand to his mouth to feed himself."

The righteous woman gazed on in sorrow, and said, "If this is, indeed, a glimpse of the world to come, then this is surely hell."

Then her guide escorted her across the hall to another large room. There, too, was a large banquet table laden with food, with hundreds of people sitting around it.

But here the people looked well fed, happy, and content.

The woman looked and saw that just as at the other banquet table, each person's arms were bound with rigid splints.

She asked her guide, "How can these people look so well fed and satisfied when their hands are bound to splints, with their arms held straight out, unable to bend to bring food to their mouths?"

The guide said, "Look carefully."

The woman looked and saw that although each person could not bend his arms to feed himself, each could grasp food in his outstretched hand, and each person could hold the food and lift it up to his neighbor's mouth. Although he could not feed himself, each person could feed his neighbor.

"If this is a glimpse of the world to come," said the woman, "then this surely is heaven."

And the guide replied, "You are right. The difference between heaven and hell is serving one's fellow human being."

You and the people of your company can help create a tiny bit of heaven here on earth when you serve your fellow human beings, when you share what you have and what you can do with those who need you.

You and your company will be active, participating, contributing members of the community where you live and work when you understand the wisdom of the saying that "service is the rent you pay for living on earth."

When you are giving away money and time, it may seem as if there is little benefit to you.

But it is not a cliché to say that "it is better to give than to receive." It is true.

As much as the causes and the people to whom you give will benefit, you and your company will gain even more.

For serving the public interest, your reputation will be enhanced, your name will be known for good.

But more important, you will feel a sense of satisfaction, a sense of happiness, a sense of well-being, a sense of doing good.

As an article in *Modern Maturity* magazine put it, "The world is full of two kinds of people: the givers and the takers. The takers eat well—but the givers sleep well."

"What goes around comes around." When you give with a full and an open heart, your gift not only gives blessing, it brings blessing back to you.

From out of the dark, dank attic in Amsterdam, where she and her family were hidden from Nazi tormentors during World War II—from out of that horrible place of distress and suffering, where she certainly could have been forgiven any despair or lament—young Anne Frank left us these words: "Give of yourself, give as much as you can! And you can always, always give something, even if it is only kindness!... Give and you shall receive, much more than you would have ever thought possible. Give, give again and again.... No one has ever become poor from giving!"

Even in her anguish and pain Anne Frank still understood that the greatest human good is giving and sharing, and that the greatest pleasure and satisfaction she herself could have would come from sharing her meager possessions and giving from the fullness of her heart.

As Kahlil Gibran explained, for "those who give with joy, joy is their reward."

The Reverend Dr. Martin Luther King, Jr., taught, "Life's most persistent and urgent question is, 'What are you doing for others?'"

There is so much to do, so many ways to work to combat the ills that beset this world, so many people and places hoping that you will come to help.

If you have been blessed with intelligence and knowledge, with talent and ability, with skill and energy, with success and with resources—and you know that you have—then you have much to give, much to share, much that you can accomplish.

There is a whole world out there just waiting for you, waiting—and needing—to make use of your resources and the work of your hands.

~

There is a whole world out there that will be enriched and ennobled—just as you will be enriched and ennobled—when you give from what you have received.

There is a whole world out there—and a whole world within your soul—that will rejoice when you understand with Muhammad that "a person's true wealth is the good he does in this world."

The Eighth Commandment

~

"REMEMBER

THE SABBATH"

Do you run your business, or does your business run you?

Why do you work? Why do you earn money?

Certainly you cherish the satisfaction of a job well done. Surely you need and want the things that money can buy.

But your job, your business, your profession, can become all-consuming. It can take up all your time, all your energy. It can seem to run your life.

Yet in all my years of visiting people in hospitals and nursing homes—people who were ill and sometimes dying—not once did any one of those people ever say to me, "Oh, Rabbi, I wish I had spent more time at work."

People said, "I wish I had spent more time with my wife, my husband, my children, my friends. I wish I had spent more time enjoying myself, doing the things that brought me pleasure and personal joy."

After an entire career of working, contributing, and earning, when you retire, the company may give you—or you may treat yourself to—a gold watch. But no matter how hard you work, how many hours you put in, how much you earn, when you die, no one is going to give you a golden tombstone.

A sage once saw a man hurrying along the street, looking neither left nor right. "Why are you rushing so?" he asked the man.

"I am pursuing my livelihood," replied the man.

"And how do you know," asked the sage, "that your livelihood is running before you, so that you have to pursue it in such a rush? Perhaps it is behind you, and all you have to do to encounter it is to stand still."

Wherever your livelihood is, once in a while it helps to stand still.

For you do your best work—you succeed the most—where you keep things in perspective, when you balance your responsibilities to work with your commitments to yourself, when you remember that you are earning a living so that you can live life.

The harder you work, the more you need to rest—to re-energize your body and to rejuvenate your soul.

When you and the people who work for and with you take off at least one day a week—not an hour or two here and there, not a once-in-a-while-if-you-can-find-the-time day, but a regularly scheduled day, which you can, if you wish, call a Sabbath—you slow down and relax, you have time to think, to contemplate, to share with the ones you love.

Your Sabbath day can enrich you enormously, because at least once each week, you tell yourself—you show yourself—what is really important to you, what really, really counts in your life.

If you are married, you can remember and keep the faith with the vows you made on your wedding day.

Once, a rabbi officiated at a funeral.

At the conclusion of the service at the cemetery, the man whose wife had just been buried stood quietly weeping over the grave.

After a few minutes the rabbi approached the man and said, "My friend, it is time to go now. It is time to leave the cemetery."

The man shook his head and said, "No, Rabbi. You don't understand."

The rabbi stepped away from the grave, giving the man a few more moments in his grief.

A few minutes later the rabbi, once again, stood next to the man. He said, "Come, my friend. It's time to go. There is nothing more that you can do here now. It's time to go now."

The man looked sadly at the rabbi and said, "No, Rabbi. You don't understand."

By this time the rabbi surmised that there was something going on beyond the normal grief and sadness that he *didn't* understand. So he said, "Tell me, my friend, what is it that I don't understand?"

The man said, "Rabbi, you don't understand. I loved my wife."

The rabbi replied, "Of course I understand that you loved your wife. But now she is gone, and there is nothing more that you can do here at the cemetery today. It's time to go home now and be with your family and friends."

The man looked at the rabbi with great anguish and deep, deep sadness, and he said, "No, Rabbi. You don't understand. I loved my wife. *And once I almost told her.*"

When you take time each week to rest and rejuvenate, you have the time to connect with the one you love.

You have the time to say the words that speak your most intimate feelings. You have the time for the gestures—large and small—that convey your love.

And if you are a parent, you can remember and fulfill the promises to the children you brought into this world.

My colleague Rabbi Jack Segal, of Houston, Texas, is a brilliant, sensitive, creative rabbi. His congregation numbers well over a thousand member families. There are programs and activities almost every moment of every day. Rabbi Segal keeps up an unbelievably hectic pace, teaching, preaching, writing, marrying, burying, creating more and more programs for his congregants.

But for Rabbi Segal there seemed never to be enough time for what he really wanted to do. Here's how he tells it.

"For all the years I have been here in Houston, it was Toby (my wife) who went to see Jeff, Mike, and Scotty play Little League baseball and watch Lisa at gymnastics. *I* was always at the synagogue. Dad, like so many other fathers, was always busy, always occupied. Events would take place at the University of Texas—Dad's Day—but the boys would always say, 'Don't feel bad, Dad. We know. We understand. You are busy at the synagogue. You can't come.'"

And then tragedy struck.

The rabbi's son Michael was buying gas for his car when a man, high on drugs, came to rob the service station. Michael, innocent bystander, was shot, and for weeks lay in a coma. He survived, but he had to undergo extensive therapy just to learn to walk again.

Rabbi Segal relates, "During those first three days, when we did not know whether he would live or die, when he did not even respond to me when I went into the ICU to hold his hand and talk to him, I would sit down and think about parents and children.

"I remembered the first time I saw my son Jeff play Little League. He was around eleven years old and playing at the park around the corner from the house. It was late Friday afternoon, and I said to Toby, 'Where's Jeff?' Toby said to me, 'Playing ball.' I said, 'It's late on Friday afternoon. It is almost sunset, time for the Sabbath to begin. I've got to eat the Sabbath meal. I've got to go over my sermon. I've got to get to the synagogue to conduct services.' Toby said to me, 'Go to the park and get Jeff.'

"I must admit that I was quite angry with Jeff. He knew that it was the Sabbath and that we always eat together before services. So I went quickly to the park, and when I got there, I noticed that Jeff's team was up at bat. I walked over to my son and said, 'Jeff, it's late. Come on home. We have to begin the Sabbath meal.'

"However, he said, 'Dad, I'm up next. Let me get my turn at bat, then I'll come home.' His eyes were pleading and tearing. I looked at my watch and said, 'Okay, but make it snappy.' And he did. He hit the first ball for a home run, and as he came across the plate, tears flowing from his eyes, he said, 'Okay, let's go home.'

"I quickly said, 'Oh, no! Stay around. You might get up again. Finish the game. Maybe you'll hit another homer.' I was so proud and happy that afternoon, and he was so elated that I remained there.

"But the next week I again had no time for Little League, and I say to you, 'What a mistake that was.'

"Only after Michael was shot did I realize the truth. It took a major tragedy to open my eyes toward my sons."

If you work too hard and don't take any time to rest and rejuvenate, your children will grow up without you. You will miss the baseball games and the ballet lessons, the Scout meetings and the piano recitals.

Instead of being like the parent in the television commercial who uses the power of his credit card to fly home to see his daughter perform in the school play, you will be like Peter in the opening scene of the movie *Hook,* rushing to his son's Little League game in between meetings and cellular phone calls, but never getting there on time.

Before you know it, your children will be all grown up, and you will be left to wonder where all the years have gone.

When you take time each week to rest and rejuvenate, you have the time to give your children the intellectual, emotional, and spiritual direction they need—the guidance they can't get from anyone but you.

And when you observe your Sabbath, you can remember the promises you made to yourself in the bright hope of your youth.

For you do not want your life to be like the one described by the modern poet:

First, I was dying to finish high school and start college.
And then I was dying to finish college and start working.
And then I was dying to marry and have children.
And then I was dying for my child to grow old enough for
    school so I could return to work.
And then I was dying to retire.
And now, I am dying…
And, suddenly, I realize I forgot to live.

When you take time each week to rest and rejuvenate, you are able to stay in touch with your own needs, your own desires, your own priorities.

You can remember what is important to you, and what you and your life are really all about. You have the time to listen to your heart, to make your choices, to set your direction, and to control your own destiny.

Already, the litany of excuses and rationalizations may be reverberating in your ears.

"I'd like to take some time off, but to get this new business off the ground I have to work eighty, ninety, a hundred hours a week."

"What kind of example will I be setting for my employees if I slack off? I've got to work, work, work."

"Time off sure sounds wonderful, but until this project is complete, we all have to work around the clock."

"Hey, I've got a family to feed, and time is money."

"Sure I'd like to have more time to spend with my kids, but I'm a single parent. I don't have anyone to count on but myself. I've got to work as much as I can so I can provide my children with all that they deserve."

"The only way to prove myself in this job is to work as much as it takes. That's what they expect. In a few years, when I make partner, then I can relax a little bit."

"I didn't go into this profession to punch a time clock. I've got responsibilities here. I've got people who need me. They come first. I'll worry about myself later."

"The only way to beat the competition is to outwork the competition. Whatever it takes, we'll do it. We'll work until we get the job done. We'll work until we win."

Is any job, any business, any profession, any assignment, any meeting, any conference, any trip, any sale, any contract, any promotion, any raise, worth sacrificing your relationship with your wife, your husband, your son, your daughter, your-self?

Is anything that happens at the office or the factory worth more than your commitments to yourself and to the ones you love?

When you listen to *both* voices within you—the voice calling you to dedicated work *and* the voice calling you to your personal commitments—you can begin to find the balance between work and relaxation, you can begin to couple your hard work with meeting your own needs, you can begin to truly understand why you work and for what you live.

How will you observe your Sabbath? What form will your Sabbath observance take?

Your Sabbath—your time for physical rest and spiritual rejuvenation—is more than merely a "weekend."

Weekends tend to be the time to rush around, trying to accomplish all the things you don't have time for during the week.

You shop, you run errands, you clean house, you do the laundry, you do home repairs, you drive the kids to their lessons and games. Then, in the few remaining hours, you "rush to relax." You try to have fun by playing a quick round of golf, or a couple of sets of tennis, by having dinner with friends, seeing a movie, or taking in a concert. You become like the American town described by the author Sherwood Anderson that "worked terribly hard at the task of amusing itself."

That weekends fail to provide the kind of rest and rejuvenation you need has now been confirmed by scientific research. A recently released study concludes that the risk of heart attack is as much as 50 percent greater on Monday than on any other day of the week!

Is it because on weekends we overindulge in food and drink? Is it because as weekend athletes we overexert? Is it because our weekend schedules are so exhausting? Is it because we become weekend couch potatoes, shutting off both brains and brawn that must be revved up again on Monday morning? Is it because we are so unhappy going back to work?

Whatever the reason, weekends—as we spend them—are literally making us vulnerable to becoming sick.

So the weekend, as we know it, is not the way for you to find the Sabbath rest and the rejuvenation that you need.

Your Sabbath can be your time to renew not only your body, but your soul.

The modern mystic Abraham Joshua Heschel taught, "The meaning of Sabbath is to celebrate time rather than space. Six days a week we live under the tyranny of things of space; on the Sabbath we try to become attuned to *holiness in time*. It is a day on which we are called upon to share in what is eternal…to turn from the *results* of creation to the *mystery* of creation…."

Perhaps you will find your renewal by participating in the structured Sabbath observance of your faith community—the Muslim Sabbath on Friday, the Jewish Sabbath on Saturday, or the Christian Sabbath on Sunday. In the calm and peace of your sanctuary, you can feel rejuvenation of spirit.

Perhaps you will find your renewal in the beauty of listening to good music or viewing fine art, in immersing in a good book, visiting a museum, or engaging in stimulating conversation. In the presence of the great creations of humankind, you can feel rejuvenation of spirit.

Perhaps you will find your renewal in the crashing waves of the seashore, in the crisp air of the mountains, in the enveloping presence of the tall trees of the forest, or in the rolling green hills of the meadow. In the awesome universe and in the wonders of nature, you can feel rejuvenation of spirit.

Your Sabbath is the time to reach to the deepest recesses of your being, to get in touch with yourself, to reconnect in body, mind, and spirit with your greatness and with your unlimited potential.

Your Sabbath, well spent, can give you a vision of your highest self, a glimpse of what you can become.

Your Sabbath, well spent, can mean that the dawning of each new day is infused with your energy, your power, and your joy.

Your Sabbath, well spent, means that you can return to your job, your business, your company, with renewed strength and renewed commitment, renewed purpose and renewed passion.

To the owners of businesses, the managers of companies, the heads of corporations, a Sabbath word.

Not for themselves and their families alone do your people observe a Sabbath day of rest.

Not for yourself and your family alone do you observe a Sabbath day of rest.

As much and more, your company can benefit from your people's rest and rejuvenation.

When you and your people are tired, stressed, and "burned-out," you are less productive, more apt to make mistakes, less passionate about your work.

But when you and your people have time to rest—to restore body and renew spirit—then enthusiasm returns, work can become more centered, new ideas can bubble up, and new determination can take hold.

For recreation is actually *re-creation.*

When they—and you—rest and rejuvenate, you can re-create yourself, you can reenergize yourself.

When they—and you—return to your tasks from your Sabbath day, you all can come back refreshed and refocused, ready for the new challenges that lie ahead.

When you provide ample time for Sabbath rest and rejuvenation, you get back from what you give out, for you are rewarded with people who have the sharpened skills and the heartfelt will to do their jobs, to do their best.

An old fable tells the story of an old farmer who was close to death. He called his two sons to his bedside and said to them, "My sons, I am now departing from this life. All that I have to leave you is to be found in my vineyard."

In but a few hours, the farmer died. Following the proper period of mourning, his two sons set out to dig up their father's vineyard, believing that he had told them of a hidden treasure that was to be found. With their spades and plows, they turned over the soil of the vineyard again and again.

They found no treasure, it is true. But the vines—strengthened and improved by this thorough tilling—yielded a finer vintage than they had ever given before, more than repaying the farmer's sons for their efforts.

Your *people* are *your* treasure.

When you give your people what they need—including the time to rest and rejuvenate, restore and renew—they will return your investment in ample measure, helping you to achieve greater and greater yield from your business.

If a weekly Sabbath of rest and rejuvenation can bring such benefit to worker and to business, then how much the more so can a *daily* Sabbath.

Each day—several times each day—you can set aside the moments to move away from the crush and the stress of work, to find refreshment and renewal.

You can designate a certain time each day—or carve out two or three ten-minute periods of time—for whatever it is that helps you connect with your inner being, and reach upward toward your higher self.

You can use whatever form, whatever technique, works best for you: Perhaps it is prayer, perhaps it is meditation, perhaps it is a specific exercise regime, perhaps it is a yoga routine, perhaps it is a few minutes of inspirational reading, perhaps it is listening to soothing music.

However you spend the minutes of your daily "mini-Sabbath," you can achieve best results when you are not casual or haphazard, but regular and consistent in your observance—when you observe your Sabbath not by aimless chance, but "religiously."

This daily mini-Sabbath can help you remain grounded and focused, well anchored in your principles and your priorities.

And at the very same time, it can give you the wings you need to soar to new heights of exploration, and new levels of achievement.

This daily mini-Sabbath can help you remember and appreciate the wisdom of the ancient Sanskrit prayer:

Look to this day!
For it is life, the very life of life.
For yesterday is already a dream,
and tomorrow is only a vision.
But, today well lived,
makes every yesterday a dream of happiness,
and every tomorrow a vision of hope.

Can you find the ten or thirty minutes in every twenty-four hours that it will take to observe your mini-Sabbath each day?

With so much to be gained, can you afford not to?

An old legend teaches that if every person would observe the Sabbath two weeks in a row, then the world would be transformed and perfected.

This is not simply a requirement of practice and observance, but a statement of atmosphere and ambience.

For if the Sabbath spirit of refreshment of body and soul, of rejuvenation and renewal, of harmony and tranquility, can be experienced two weeks in a row—and presumably for all the days in between, for how could that glorious a mood be shattered?—then worldly perfection will have arrived.

Can you imagine how much happier and more satisfied you and your people will be when you observe your Sabbath week after week?

Can you imagine what incredible accomplishment and success your business will experience when you and your people sustain your Sabbath feelings day after day?

An impossible dream? An inconceivable vision?

Not if you remember the words of Bobby Kennedy, who was fond of quoting George Bernard Shaw: "Some people see things as they are and say, 'Why?' I dream things that never were and say, 'Why not?'"

You are the dream and the dreamer, the vision and the visionary.

You are deliverer of the promise of the Sabbath, assuring growth and renewal.

You are the power of the message of the Sabbath, enveloping the marketplace.

You are the bearer of the spirit of the Sabbath, transforming the world of business.

As you observe your Sabbaths and convey their majesty, may your Sabbaths—in the words of the modern prayer— "give purpose to your work, meaning to your struggle and direction to your striving." May your Sabbaths "bring peace to your heart, and strengthen you for the days and the weeks that lie ahead."

The Ninth Commandment

~

"ACQUIRE

WISDOM"

When I was in high school, I had a favorite English teacher.

She was young and beautiful (qualities much appreciated by a teenage boy), and she was challenging, demanding, and inspiring (qualities much appreciated, only in retrospect, by that teenage boy now become a man).

We all knew that she had once dated a handsome young man, for she told us of their adventures at the movies and the theater, going ice skating in the winter, and taking long walks on warm summer nights.

But there had been something about this young man that was very strange and very troubling to our teacher.

He seemed to just disappear on Wednesdays.

Every other day of the week, he was available for a date, for dinner, for a phone call. But on Wednesdays he was never around.

He never came to pick her up after school on Wednesday afternoons, he never made a date for Wednesday evenings, he never answered his phone on Wednesday nights.

Our teacher began to worry: Was he secretly married? Did he have a date with another woman? Did he play cards with his friends and gamble away a lot of money? Was he engaged in some illegal activity?

Why was he never available on Wednesdays?

She asked, but he would not tell her. She invited him to Wednesday dinners, but he would not come. She bought tickets to Wednesday concerts and ball games, but he would not go. No matter what she did, her handsome young man simply would not reveal where he was or what he was doing on Wednesdays.

Finally, exasperated—and a little scared—our teacher issued an ultimatum: Either tell me where you are and what you are doing on Wednesdays, or I'm breaking off our relationship.

He did not want to lose her (for teenage boys were not the only ones who appreciated her beauty and charm), so reluctantly, and with much embarrassment, he explained.

He was, as he had told her, a salesman for a national brand-name table wine. All week he went from client to client—stores, restaurants, and bars—selling his wine.

On Wednesdays the company brought the entire sales force together for lunch to give weekly sales reports and hear motivational talks. The luncheon was catered at the company headquarters and, of course, always included glasses of wine—the product the company was selling.

Surrounded by all his bosses and his fellow salesmen, the man was obligated to eat the lunch and, certainly, drink the wine he was served.

But, he reported, drinking the wine made him so sick that he had to go home and get into bed every Wednesday afternoon.

All week long this man spent all his working hours going from client to client selling wine that he touted as a good-tasting, high-quality vintage. But the one day a week that he was forced to drink his own wine, he became seriously ill.

This man made his living by selling a product that made him throw up!

How sad it must have been for him to go to work every day to sell a product he hated, to lie his way through every sales call, to have all his working hours and efforts mean nothing more to him than a paycheck at the end of the week.

It is true, as the old axiom teaches, that money is a powerful motivator: "Another day, another dollar."

That is why, every working day, for forty years or more, you wake up, get dressed, and go to your job, your business, your profession. You need to earn a living, to provide yourself and your family with the necessities—and hopefully a few of the luxuries—of life.

But is money enough?

When you spend the days of your *entire lifetime* at work, don't you want more than a paycheck?

Wouldn't you like your work to be exciting and meaningful enough to you that you are eager to get out of bed every morning?

Do you remember hearing about the mother who came into her son's bedroom to wake him up?

She said, "Time to get up. Time to get ready for school."

Her son pulled the covers up over his face and said, "I'm not going to school this morning."

His mother asked, "Why aren't you going to school? Are you sick?"

"No, I'm not sick," her son replied, "but I'm not going to school."

"If you're not sick, why aren't you going to school?"

"I'm not going to school because I don't like it there. The kids hate me and the teachers hate me, and I'm not going anymore."

Pulling the covers off him, his mother said, "It doesn't matter if the kids hate you and the teachers hate you. You're forty years old and you're the principal. Get up. You're going to school."

Wouldn't you like your work to be worth getting up for? Wouldn't you like your work to give you a continuing sense of happiness and self-esteem, of accomplishment and satisfaction?

How do you do it? How do you find and sustain work that compensates you fairly and decently and is, at the same time, worthwhile and meaningful to you?

The contemporary teacher Marsha Sinetar advises, "Do what you love, the money will follow."

You can choose work that you like and gives you pleasure. You can choose work that is important, that gives you deep personal fulfillment. You can choose work that touches people's lives, that gives you a sense that you are making a real contribution to the world in which you live.

The good news is that the satisfaction that you seek can be found in any work you choose.

In medicine there can be the satisfaction of healing and saving lives, and in trash collecting there can be the satisfaction of keeping the community clean and healthy. In air control there can be the satisfaction of maintaining safe skies, and in law enforcement there can be the satisfaction of preserving safe streets.

In accounting there can be the satisfaction of balancing numbers, in waiting tables there can be the satisfaction of feeding hungry people, in construction there can be the satisfaction of building houses where families make homes.

In research there can be the satisfaction of uncovering mysteries, in performing there can be the satisfaction of unleashing laughter and tears, in driving a truck there can be the satisfaction of delivering the goods on time.

In sales there can be the satisfaction of giving people what they want, in teaching there can be the satisfaction of sharing what you know, in fashion design there can be the satisfaction of creating what you dream.

In every single job, in every single business, in every single profession—in *whatever* you do—there can be the satisfaction and the happiness that comes from knowing that what you do is important, that what you do makes a difference in the lives of the people you serve.

Every working moment won't be fun. There will always be problems and frustrations and stress.

But if, on balance, the good outweighs the bad, accomplishment outweighs the drudgery, and happiness outweighs the hassles, then your work can be worthy of your energy and your commitment, your work can be worthwhile.

If, at the end of most days, you can say to yourself, "What I did today made a difference, what I did today made a contribution, what I did today makes me feel good," then your work can have meaning, your work life can bring you contentment and joy.

But what happens if your job is boring and dreary? What happens if you dread getting up every morning because you think that your work is insignificant and unimportant? What happens if your work brings you little sense of satisfaction or fulfillment? What happens if your job is not something you *want* to do, but something you *have* to do because you really need the money?

What happens if you go to work *just* to get a paycheck?

An answer may come from a bumper sticker recently seen

on a dump truck: "Don't laugh. One daughter at Berkeley. One daughter at Stanford. Dad has to work."

The driver-father accepts his workaday role with good grace and good humor because the purpose for which he works—earning the money to pay for his children's education—is more important and rewarding to him than any dislike he might have of the job he does.

And who knows? A man with the kind of offbeat humor to make up such a bumper sticker may very well *love* driving his truck—or has learned to *tolerate* driving his truck—spending happy days on his appointed rounds, knowing what the results of his labors will bring.

On the Jewish New Year—the holiday of Rosh Hashanah—the main ritual of the worship service is the sounding of the shofar, the ram's horn, which calls people to remembrance and repentance.

One day the rabbi was interviewing candidates to blow the shofar in the synagogue on the holiday. He asked each one, "What will you be thinking about when you sound the shofar on the holy day?"

The first man said, "I will be thinking about the glory of God."

The second man said, "I will be thinking about the enormity of sin."

The third man said, "I will be thinking about the money I will earn, for my children are hungry and I need to buy them food."

Who got the job?

The man who *needed* the job, for that man was the one who would bring the most sincerity, the most passion, the greatest sense of urgency and personal fulfillment to his holy task.

There can be great honor—and there can be great personal satisfaction—in doing "an honest day's work for an honest day's pay," in joyfully accepting responsibility and obligation, in using your work to meet your needs.

In freely admitting that you work not necessarily because you *want* to but because you *have* to, you have one of two choices.

You can slough off and try to "just get by," doing as little as possible in order to get your paycheck.

Or you can give yourself the opportunity to derive great *personal* meaning and fulfillment from your work.

For you can work not for "outside" recognition, not for "outside" approval, but for "inner" satisfaction, for "inner" reward.

You can have the satisfaction of knowing that you do the very, very best job you can do. You can have the integrity and the joy of knowing that you give 100 percent of your energy, your capability, your dedication, to your work.

If you mop floors, you can have the cleanest floors. If you design rocket boosters, you can have the most meticulous drawings. If you stock shelves, you can have the straightest displays. If you attach car doors on an assembly line, you can align the doors perfectly. If you manage multimillion-dollar stock portfolios, you can buy and sell with total integrity. If you clean houses, you can have the neatest houses on the block.

If you are part of a work team, you can contribute your very best work, for you know that a team is only as strong as its weakest member. The orchestra produces magnificent sound only when every instrument is played precisely by every musician. The chorus produces beautiful music only when every singer hits each note in perfect harmony. Your team, your unit, your division, can produce and succeed only when you give your best skills and your strongest commitment.

Everything depends on you being sure that you are doing your best.

For when you bring to your work your best effort, you can derive the most satisfaction.

I remember attending a high school track meet. I watched runners from a number of different schools compete in a long race—several times around the track. As the runners raced on, one runner fell farther and farther behind.

The winner crossed the finish line, all the other runners completed the race, and this one runner was still making his way around the track.

Finally he finished the race—far, far behind all the other competitors. Immediately he rushed over to his coach who held the stopwatch. He glanced at the watch, and then began jumping up and down, yelling and screaming in great happiness.

"I did my PB," he cried out. "I did my PB, my Personal Best."

Even though he had finished far behind every other runner, this young man was elated. He had run his race in his own personal best time ever. He had achieved his own personal best score.

All the practice, all the sweat, all the sore muscles, were worth it. He was satisfied, personally fulfilled, and very, very happy.

Whatever you do, you can do with excellence, with pride, and with satisfaction.

The fate of civilization may not depend on the quality of elastic in the waistbands of men's underwear, but Inspector Number 12 feels a great sense of personal pride and the glow of inner satisfaction when she says, "It doesn't say 'Hanes' until *I* say it says 'Hanes.'"

Albert Camus once wrote, "In the midst of winter, I finally learned that there was, in me, an invincible summer."

In you is the happiness and joy of incredible summer.

In you—in your heart and in your soul—is all the satisfaction, all the importance, all the meaning, you will ever need from your work.

In the words of the popular song, "Just open up your heart and let the sun shine in."

What do you do when you are fairly content at your job, when the money is good enough, but when the circumstances of your business or conditions of the economy turn sour?

What do you do if you are handed a pink slip and told that there is no more work for you?

A generation ago choice of work was most often a lifetime decision. Operating a business or going to work for a particular company was most often a lifetime commitment.

Not anymore.

In the middle 1970s and into the 1980s, when defense contracts were being significantly modified and America's space program was being greatly changed, entire towns full of defense-industry workers and aerospace engineers were laid off. At midcareer these men and women had to find not only new jobs but entirely new careers.

In the late 1980s and into the 1990s, the auto industry closed plants across the country. Assembly-line workers, middle managers, and high-level executives all had to search for work, and learn to adapt their skills to new endeavors.

Even the giant IBM, the granddaddy of all companies known for giving job security to its workers, was forced to offer early retirement to tens of thousands of employees—some with twenty and more years of service and deep loyalty to Big Blue. What do you do if you have given half a lifetime of midlevel management to a company—where you began and where you assumed you would end your working career—when the company tells you it no longer has a place for you?

Or what do you do when the job, the business, the profession, that originally brought you happiness and satisfaction is no longer enough for you?

The old excitement is missing; the old joy is gone. The old sense of accomplishment and fulfillment has disappeared.

Sometimes even the money is not enough.

You want more.

It is then when—out of necessity or out of choice—you can follow your dream.

Today most workers will change jobs six or seven times in the course of a lifetime, and may change whole careers once or twice.

So you can begin by asking yourself: What do I really want to do? How do I want to spend my days? What kind of work will give me the most happiness, the most satisfaction, the most joy?

Perhaps you want to modify your original plans and alter your original path, to make your own choices rather than follow company-imposed decisions, to opt for choice of lifestyle rather than so-called career advancement.

The television cartoon character Bart Simpson wore a T-shirt that said, "I'm an Under-Achiever and Proud of It!"

You do not have to be an underachiever, but you don't have to be an overachiever either.

"Who is rich?" asked the sage. "The person who is happy, who is content, with his own portion."

Not long ago one of the only ways to enhance your career, to move up the company hierarchy, to make more money, was to move along from job to job—two years at this task, eighteen months at that, three years at another—which often meant moving your family from city to city, from home to home.

Now some people are beginning to say, "I am perfectly happy with the job I have, the tasks I do. I like my work. I like the community in which I live. I don't want to move my family around from place to place, my children from school to school. I am willing to forgo new titles and higher income for stability and contentment. I want to do my work well—constantly growing and evolving in capability and contribution—but I am satisfied to be where I am, doing what I am doing, and I really don't want anything more."

Perhaps it is time in your life for radical change, for giving up what you are doing now in order to do what you really want to do.

I know a highly successful corporate attorney who gave up his prestigious practice and six-figure income to take courses in photography and journalism. He now writes and takes pictures for a local newspaper for a fraction of his former salary, but with a new energy for life and a wide grin on his face.

Conversely, I know a woman who worked as a clerk in offices for the past fifteen years. She dreamed of being a lawyer. First she had to finish undergraduate courses, which she had deferred more than a decade ago. Then she had to get accepted by a law school, and take all her classes at night—because she still had to go to work every day to support herself and her child. Today she is a proud and very happy new attorney, specializing in worker-compensation cases.

I know a schoolteacher who quit to take acting classes, and I know a clothing store owner who is now a carpenter. I know a minister who now sells real estate, and I know a stockbroker who repairs sailboats. I know a college professor who became a literary agent, and I know a physicist who tunes pianos.

Some people are following their heart's desires by leaving jobs where they work for others, and opening businesses of their own.

In the age-old entrepreneurial spirit, these people are willing to take the risks in order to reap the potential rewards—to control their own destinies and shape their own futures.

Others are opening businesses that embody a particular vision—a political viewpoint or a social consciousness. Called "social entrepreneurs," these new business owners create companies that reflect their strong convictions and their sincerely held beliefs.

Following the dictates of their conscience, these new business people sell clothing made only of natural fiber, or open a restaurant that has only vegetarian food on the menu, or operate a farm that grows only pesticide-free organic vegetables, or open a recycling center, or establish a mail-order-catalog business that sells vitamins and health care products.

For these business pioneers, the marketplace has become a reflection of their ethical values, a place where their world of business and their world of the spirit can comfortably converge.

Whatever it is, wherever it leads you, you can follow your dream, you can *live* your dream.

The only thing that is stopping you is the litany of "if onlys" that is playing in your head: "*If only* I had accumulated enough money to be able to take this chance…" "*If only* I had the educational background…" "*If only* the mortgage were paid off…" "*If only* I were married / weren't married / had a relationship / weren't in this relationship…" "*If only* my kid's college tuition didn't cost so much…" "*If only* I had put more money into the company pension plan…" "*If only* I had more time…" "*If only* I had more courage…" "*If only…if only…if only…*"

Rabbi Bunam (remember him?) used to tell the story of Rabbi Eisik, the son of Rabbi Yekel, of Cracow.

After many years of great poverty, Rabbi Eisik dreamed that he was bidden to go to Prague to look for a treasure, which was under the bridge leading to the king's palace. After dreaming the same dream night after night, Rabbi Eisik set out for Prague to uncover his treasure.

But when he arrived in Prague, he saw that the bridge was guarded day and night. He could not start digging for his treasure, lest he be discovered. Nevertheless, he went to the bridge every morning and kept walking around it until late at night.

Finally the captain of the guards asked him, in a very kindly way, if he were looking for something or waiting for someone.

Rabbi Eisik told him his story—that he had come to Prague from Cracow, bidden by his dream to search for his treasure under the king's bridge.

The captain laughed and said, "Ah, poor fellow. To please a dream, you wore out your shoes to come here. As for having faith in dreams, if I had it, I would follow my dream—the dream that I dream night after night—and go to Cracow to dig for my treasure under the stove of the Jew Eisik, the son of Yekel. But I can just imagine how impossible that would be. I would have to try every house over there, for half the Jews must be named Eisik and the other half must be named Yekel." And he laughed again.

Rabbi Eisik said farewell to the captain, traveled home, and dug up his treasure right from under his very own stove.

Your treasure is not far away; your dream is far from impossible.

Your treasure is right where you are.

Your dream is right in you.

You *can* follow your dream to new meaning, new satisfaction, new happiness in your work and in your life.

Seeking meaning and value in work need not be a worker's task alone.

Bosses and businesses, companies and corporations can help their people tremendously in finding and fostering personal satisfaction in the workplace.

Chroniclers of contemporary business excellence Tom Peters and Robert Waterman, in their book *In Search of Excellence*, point to a number of companies that purposefully create a corporate climate encouraging and rewarding personal innovation, initiative, and growth.

Some of the best product ideas in recent years have come not through normal research-and-development channels but from what are called "skunk works"—"bands of eight or ten zealots off in the corner"—people who are given the time, the space, and the opportunity to pursue their ideas and follow their hunches.

When you give your people the freedom to use their own imagination, to tinker and to create, your company benefits not only from the resulting products but also from the presence of happy, satisfied workers who feel pride in their accomplishment and appreciated for their contribution.

To create a workplace that encourages personal satisfaction and nurtures the need for meaningful work, some companies have established affinity groups, based on the Japanese model of creating a familylike atmosphere in the business setting—a group of intertwined workers striving toward a common goal.

While there is much benefit—and there has been much success—in groups that develop a sense of mutual participation, responsibility, and achievement, the caution is that the American culture of family-centered personal liberty is different from the Japanese culture of business-based loyalty.

While an American worker begins to feel closer and closer to his team partners at work, there is the chance that his wife and children, who are left in the suburbs, at the other end of his long daily commute, will begin to feel further and further alienated from their husband and father and his job. The benefits that are gained at work can be easily nullified by the problems created at home.

In seeking ways to foster meaning and satisfaction in the workplace, your company can best succeed when you tailor your programs to the specific needs and mindsets of your people.

Some companies encourage worker satisfaction by providing a mentoring program.

An ancient sage advised, "Get yourself a teacher."

There is always more to learn, old wisdom to tap, experience from which to benefit, wise perceptions to gain.

It does not matter if you are just starting out, if you are a longtime veteran, if you are the boss or the owner. There is always something new you can learn, new insight you can acquire.

You can benefit from all the accumulated wisdom of the past. You can be introduced to the new advances being made, the new techniques being perfected.

Your company can offer each worker a teacher who is a mentor and a guide.

As your mentor model, you can use the social-work profession, where every social worker, no matter how skilled, no matter how advanced, always has a supervisor as a teaching guide.

The supervisor provides *super vision,* seeing the "big picture," facilitating process, and helping to articulate goals.

And the supervisor with *super vision* is a sounding board, a mirror, who can reflect back your thoughts and ideas, who can help you see yourself. With a look in the mirror of *super vision,* not only can your work grow through you, but you can grow through your work.

By providing opportunities for ongoing learning, your

company can vividly demonstrate your commitment to the personal growth of your people.

Beyond in-house mentoring, your company can support personal growth through continuing education by providing for formal educational opportunities for your people.

Some companies offer time and funds for their people to attend college.

Some companies pay tuition costs for their people to study for advanced degrees in their fields.

Some companies encourage and pay for their people to take courses in fields unrelated to their work—for enrichment and personal growth. A scientist takes courses in music appreciation; an accountant takes courses in philosophy; a salesman takes courses in comparative literature; a CEO takes courses in applied physics; an assembly-line worker takes courses in art history.

The opportunity to increase knowledge and expand horizons helps contribute to the growth, self-esteem, and happiness of your people.

Some companies have programs for new learning and growth as part of the business day.

When he won a Pulitzer Prize for political investigative journalism at a midwestern newspaper, a reporter was asked, "What new project would you like to work on now?" He replied, "I've always loved baseball. I'd like to cover our baseball team this season." So for the next six months, this internationally famed political journalist wrote a sports column.

A top sales rep for a clothing manufacturer asked for a three-month internship in her company's advertising department. She is quickly on her way to becoming a brilliantly creative marketer.

In another company a vice president for product

development asked to be transferred back to his old lab for a little while. After returning to his roots and doing pure scientific research for a few months, he returned to his executive office refreshed and renewed, ready to meet new challenges with a fresh eye.

When you have the vision and the courage to shake up the corporate ladder a little bit, to try the untried, to let your people test their own abilities and experiment with their own careers, you can have happier, more fulfilled people, and, most likely, your company will benefit from the new capabilities and the new talents your people discover in themselves.

You can offer your people even wider opportunities to enhance their skills and expand their worlds.

Some companies offer their people sabbaticals—extended periods of paid time off to learn, to travel, to give service, to grow. If sabbaticals are good for academia and the clergy, they are good for business. The time and the support to pursue personal projects and follow personal dreams is repaid many times over by workers who return to their companies inspired and reenergized.

Some companies pay full salary and benefits to their workers who are on sabbatical. A few companies follow the model offered to federal employees by the Canadian government. Instead of taking full income each year, the worker takes 80 percent of salary. In the fifth year of the program, the worker gets the entire year off as sabbatical, at 80 percent salary. Even though the fifth-year salary is really his own money—earned but deferred over the previous four years—the availability of such a program encourages many to take advantage of the life-enhancing sabbatical experience.

This Canadian program can serve as an outstanding model of cooperation between companies and their people which, ultimately, can be of great benefit to both.

Some companies help structure sabbatical time by assisting their people in finding challenging, exciting and fulfilling ways to serve their communities. So, for example, the head of the public relations department at a major company is spending this year teaching communications to freshmen at a local community college. The employee is enriched by his year of teaching, the students learn from an experienced professional, and the company, the college and the community have formed a mutually beneficial partnership.

Everyone wins.

In order to make best use of every single one of its people, many companies have appointed representatives to foster open, ongoing and candid communications between labor and management.

Called vice president for human resources or ombudsman or company-employee liaison, these representatives are the links between a company and its people.

All too often, traditional performance reviews are potentially confrontational and adversarial. An employee might be afraid to speak the whole truth, in fear of intimidation or repercussion. The evaluator might be reticent to speak the whole truth, in fear of hurting feelings, increasing tension, or creating ill will. Everyone might be cautious about speaking the whole truth because of the legalities governing employer-employee relationships, and the consequences of violating those rules.

Yet great ideas may be left unspoken, great talent may be going to waste, great frustration may be growing, when feelings and needs are not freely and honestly spoken.

So the company liaison, who (no easy task) must gain the trust and the confidence of both the employer and the employee—becomes the advocate for the employee with the company and for the company with the employee.

An employee who thinks that her talents are being wasted because she knows that she can handle much more complex tasks has a place to talk and be heard. An employee who thinks that his supervisor is stifling his creativity has a place to talk and be heard. An employee who thinks that her suggestions are being thoughtlessly dismissed has a place to talk and be heard.

A company's greatest resource is its people.

When people are heard, when talent and skills are best utilized, when each individual is respected and appreciated, frustration and tension can go down, happiness and satisfaction, productivity and profits, can go up.

These—and the hundreds of other strategies that are being established and implemented in companies throughout the business world—can be seen as the signal of the growing partnership between workers who seek meaning and fulfillment in their work, and businesses that want happy, satisfied, productive workers.

Everyone's best interest can best be served when there is a unity of purpose, when personal needs are joined with professional goals.

In *In Search of Excellence,* Peters and Waterman tell of the Foxboro company where, in the early days, a particular technical advance was desperately needed.

One day a scientist rushed into the president's office with a working prototype.

The president was overjoyed with the discovery, and wanted to offer an immediate, tangible sign of his gratitude. Rummaging on his desk, he grabbed the only thing he had to give—the leftover dessert from his lunch, a banana. He spontaneously thrust it at the scientist and said, "Here, have a banana."

From then on, the "Gold Banana," which is now a lapel pin, is one of the highest honors acknowledging creativity and innovation that this company can give.

A hundred times a day—literally and figuratively—you have the opportunity to give your people a "gold banana"—recognition of excellence and acknowledgment of achievement.

You can create a workplace that supports growth, and helps build pathways toward personal happiness and satisfaction.

You can create a workplace that encourages your people to find value and worth in their tasks, meaning and fulfillment in their work.

You can create a workplace that respects your people and honors their dreams, a workplace that celebrates their uniqueness and rewards their contributions.

In a suburban restaurant, a waitress welcomed every customer with a warm greeting and a wide smile.

She knew her people, and when one of her "regular" families came in, as they were hanging up their coats, she had decaf coffee on the table for Mom, orange juice for Dad, a diet soda and a chocolate milkshake for the kids. She knew their preferences, and brought their drinks even before they sat down.

No matter how busy she was, she always had time for a short chat—asking about the children's progress in school, remembering special family occasions, expressing interest in family activities.

Her tables were always full because people kept coming back to be served by this friendly, extraordinarily competent waitress.

One day a longtime customer said to her, "Waitressing is hard work. Yet you always seem so friendly, so happy. How do you do it? How do you have the time and the energy to remember all your customers, know what they want to eat and drink, and spend a special moment with each one?"

She said, "You're right. Being a waitress is very hard work. So rather than let it get me down and rather than feeling sorry for myself, I go to work every day and wait for my family to come by. I consider you all to be part of my family, and I'm so happy to see you when you come to visit me."

Wouldn't it be incredible if each and every one of your people considered coming to work to be like a pleasant visit with family?

Wouldn't it be incredible if each and every one of your people felt joy and happiness at coming to work each day?

Wouldn't it be incredible if you could create the kind of supportive environment where each and every one of your people can feel satisfied and content?

The "incredible" can become the reality when you understand the words of the Chinese proverb: "When you plant for a year, plant grass. When you plant for ten years, plant trees. When you plant for centuries, plant people."

Educator Steven Helfgot counsels high school and college students about career choices.

He asks, "What do you want to be?"

The students reply, "I want to be a doctor. I want to be a computer programmer. I want to be a secretary. I want to be an engineer. I want to be a teacher."

Dr. Helfgot tells his students they are giving the *right* answers to the *wrong* question. They are answering the question, "What do you want *to do?*"

Work is not *who you are.*

Work is *what you do.*

That is why I never say, "I am a rabbi," or "I am a teacher," or "I am a writer." I say, "I rabbi. I teach. I write."

Helfgot cautions against getting caught up in believing that what you do is who you are, for you can always lose your job, but—if you keep things in proper perspective—you won't ever lose yourself.

Yet what you do is a vital ingredient in the formula of human existence, an essential component of your being.

Through your work, you can find meaning and value in your life, you can grow and evolve as a human being, you can feel personal satisfaction and experience deep happiness from what you accomplish.

Through your work, you can achieve your noblest ambitions and sustain your greatest dreams.

Through your work, you can touch the finest within yourself.

Through your work, you can come to understand the good counsel of the modern writer Leo Rosten, who teaches, "The purpose of life is...to matter, to be productive, to be useful, to have it make some difference that you lived at all."

And through your work, you can make this ancient entreaty your own: "Teach me to make good account of my days, that I may acquire a heart of wisdom."

The Tenth Commandment

~

"KNOW BEFORE

WHOM YOU

STAND"

When Lyndon Johnson was president of the United States, one of his aides was Bill Moyers, now of television fame, but then a political consultant and originally an ordained Baptist minister.

One day, at a luncheon at the White House, Johnson asked Moyers to give the prayer before the meal.

Moyers began his prayer, but Johnson, who was sitting at the other end of the table, couldn't hear. So he shouted, "Speak up, Bill. I can't hear you."

And Moyers replied, "Mr. President, I wasn't talking to you."

Who is your boss? To whom do you answer? Who has the power? Who makes the final decisions? Who holds the ultimate authority?

Is it your customer, who orders from you? Is it your supervisor, who gives you your assignments? Is it the owner, who signs your checks? Is it the board of directors, who must ratify your decisions? Is it the stockholders, who must approve your plan? Is it yourself, on whom all responsibility falls?

No matter who it may be, no matter what person seems to control your fate and your destiny, there is something else that is your real boss, something else that fashions your work and molds your conduct.

There is something beyond you, something greater than you, that defines and shapes you, that sets out for you standards of right and wrong, that demands your goodness and calls you to greatness.

Some people call it intuition. Some call it gut feeling. Some call it conscience. Some call it the inner force. Some call it the higher spirit.

Some call it God.

No matter what you call it, it is always present, summoning you to heed its commands.

And you are always in its presence, compelling you to know before whom you stand.

When you know before whom you stand, you can know who you are.

Not long ago, I was at the airport waiting for a flight.

All of a sudden, a policeman came up to a woman and a four- or five-year-old girl who were waiting for the same plane.

The policeman said to the woman, "I know that this will seem strange, but a four-and-a-half-year-old girl has disappeared. The description given by her parents very much fits this little girl—curly blonde hair, blue eyes, wearing a red dress and black shoes. I don't want to alarm you, but I am going to have to ask you some questions to prove that this little girl is really yours, that she isn't the little girl who is missing."

What a situation!

The woman had to prove that her daughter was really her daughter.

The policeman asked the woman's name, address, hometown, and husband's name. Then he said to the little girl, "What's your name?"

"Mary," she said.

"What's your last name?"

Silence.

"Well, where do you live?"

"At home."

"Do you know the name of your city?"

"Nope."

"What's your daddy's name?" he asked.

"Daddy."

"What does your daddy do?"

"He goes to work."

Since he wasn't getting anywhere with the little girl, the policeman turned back to the woman. "Do you have any pictures of your little girl in your wallet? Any pictures of your husband that your girl might recognize?"

"No," she said, "I don't carry any pictures."

"Well, what about your plane tickets? Let me see your plane tickets."

"We're on standby," she said, "We don't have our tickets yet."

So, what would you do? How would you prove that your child is actually your child? How would you prove that the little girl or boy with you isn't someone else's child whom you've kidnapped?

Frightening, isn't it?

Eventually the policeman must have been satisfied, because he apologized for the intrusion and left.

If only he had been able to hear the dialogue immediately following his departure, there would have been no problem in the first place.

"Mommy, Mommy," cried the little girl, "what did that man want from us?"

But the incident got me to thinking. How would I have identified my young sons (oh, those many years ago) if I had been in the same situation? What could we have done to prove that we are actually father and son?

If I had had the presence of mind to think clearly in that scary moment, the answer would have been fairly easy. I would have said, "Scott, tell the policeman what we say before we eat."

And Scott would have said—first in Hebrew and then in English—"Praised are You, O Lord our God, who brings forth bread from the earth."

And then I would have said, "Seth, tell the policeman what we say before we go to bed at night."

And Seth would have said—first in Hebrew and then in English—"Hear, O Israel, the Lord is our God, the Lord is One."

And the policeman would have known that these are my sons.

When you know before whom you stand, you know your identity and your purposes, you know your values and your commitments.

When you know before whom you stand, you can be guided to do your best.

Recently, at a baseball game, I heard a youngster cheering on his favorite player, all-star outfielder Dave Winfield.

I expected the young boy to yell, "Hit a homer, Dave," or, at the very least, "Get a hit, Dave."

But instead this young man—well trained in the art of the possible—called out, "Do your best, Dave. Do your best."

The ancient sage Zusya once said, "If they ask me in the next world 'Why were you not as devout as Abraham, as faithful as Moses, as wise as King Solomon?' I will know what to say.

"But if they ask me 'Why were you not the best Zusya?' I will have nothing to say."

When you know before whom you stand—in the dark of the night, or in the light of the mirror reflecting yourself to yourself—you will know whether you did your best.

When you know before whom you stand, you can be guided to do right.

When you know before whom you stand, every contact and every contract, every dealing and every deal, can stand up to the scrutiny of the all-seeing eye that is your conscience or your God.

It can be difficult and confusing to do right, to do good—to accept a moral mandate and live up to an established standard of ethical behavior—when definitions, circumstances, and situations seem constantly changing and subject to personal interpretation.

Yet as the modern mystic Abraham Joshua Heschel taught, "Man's understanding of *what* is right and wrong has often varied throughout the ages; yet the consciousness that *there is* a distinction between right and wrong is permanent and universal."

And modern technology has conveniently provided a measuring stick by which you can determine whether or not you are conducting your business in an acceptable, ethical way.

You can ask yourself: How will I feel if my business dealings today become tomorrow morning's newspaper headlines?

You can ask yourself: How will I feel if my business dealings today are secretly recorded on a hidden video camera, and appear on this evening's television newscast for all to see?

Have you acted in a way that will bring embarrassment?

The celebrated American author Mark Twain noted that "man is the only animal that blushes—or needs to."

Or have you acted in a way that you will be proud for your neighbors, your mother, and your children to see?

Would the Wall Street insider traders have acted any differently if they had known that their faces would be on the covers of national newsmagazines?

Would the takeover deal makers or the union-management contract negotiators have behaved any differently if they had known that their bargaining would become the subject of full-length books?

Would the Los Angeles policemen have treated Rodney King any differently if they had known that their actions were being recorded for international broadcast?

Will you conduct your business—how you treat your people, how you bargain and negotiate, how you make your deals, how you count your money—as if all that you do is open to the light of public examination?

Will you do what is good?

Will you do what is right?

Will you go the one step further? Will you embrace the teaching of the modern philosopher who did not care about newspaper headlines or videotapes and taught, "I am honest because I want to be honest with myself, not because you or anyone else exists."

You have—in the words of the title of the television soap opera—only one life to live.

Will you live your life in never-ending fear of being discovered for your misdeeds, continually looking back over your shoulder, constantly haunted in sleep?

Will you come to the end of your life, will you come to that intimate moment of personal judgment, and—with great longing and regret—be forced to say, "I blew it"?

Or will you be able to live your life openly and honestly, in full public view, staunch in your integrity and faithful to your trust?

Will you be able to shape the quality and the character of your life through goodness and truth?

When you know before whom you stand—in the places where excuses and rationalizations give way to your absolute honesty, and in the place where you see yourself with complete candor—you will know whether you did right.

When you know before whom you stand, you can know that you are never alone.

When the father of the holy Baal Shem Tov—the founder of Judaism's Hasidic movement—was about to die, he took his young son into his arms and said, "My time has come, and it has not been permitted to me to rear you to manhood.

"But, my precious son, remember all your days that your God is with you, around you, and beside you whenever you call upon Him.

"And because of this, you need fear nothing in all this world."

No matter how wise and talented you are, no matter how experienced you are, no matter how confident you are, your job, your business, will present you with situations that are hard to handle, problems that are hard to solve, decisions that are difficult to make, crises that demand immediate—and usually, very creative—solutions.

Sometimes it seems as if the burdens and the responsibilities fall on you, and you alone. The tasks seem overwhelming, and the pressures almost too much to bear.

But you are never alone.

When you know before whom you stand, you can meet any challenge, face any fear, and overcome any obstacle, for the courage, the strength, and the help you need, not merely to endure but to prevail, is always with you.

When you know before whom you stand, you can know that within you is a spark of the Divine.

Long, long ago, when the Holy Temple was still standing in Jerusalem, a man came to the high priest.

He said, "I would like to enter into the Holy of Holies, the most sacred place in the entire Temple. There, I would like to meet God."

The high priest said to him, "I am sorry, but only I—only the high priest—can enter into the Holy of Holies. This awesome role has come to me not through my own merit, but through heredity. For the office of high priest once belonged to my father. Now it is mine, and one day my son shall inherit it from me.

"I understand your great desire to enter into the Holy of Holies, but it is just not possible."

But the man was persistent. Over and over again he asked; over and over again he begged.

Finally the high priest—more to rid himself of the man than anything else—said, "All right. I will see to it that you are able to enter into the Holy of Holies. But first you must prove your sincerity. For the next *twenty* years, you must serve here in the Temple. You will sweep the floors and take out the garbage. You will assist the priests with all their duties and do whatever is required of you. In that way you will prove your worth and earn your visit into the Holy of Holies."

Of course, the priest thought that the man would soon tire of his chores. But much to his surprise—and growing worry—

year after year, the man faithfully carried out all his assigned tasks.

Twenty years passed, and the man came to the high priest. He said, "I have done all that you have required. I have served you and the other priests in love and devotion for all these years. Now the time has come. I am ready to enter the Holy of Holies."

The high priest had no choice. He had to keep his word and fulfill his promise. He said to the man, "Pray and fast for the next three days in preparation for entering the Holy of Holies. Then you shall enter into the holy place to meet your God."

At the end of the three days, the high priest dressed the man in the finest of white clothing. He led him to the door of the sacred sanctuary and said to him, "Open this door and walk through it. On the other side, you will enter into the Holy of Holies, the place where you will meet your God."

The man opened the door, walked through, and found himself—outside, in the streets of Jerusalem.

He stood among the people who were going about their everyday tasks—trading in the open-air market and hurrying off to do their work. He saw families gathered around their tables sharing a meal, and he saw little children learning in their schools.

And the man realized how wise the high priest had been. His God is not in any one place, set apart from people. He is in the midst of people, and a part of their lives. He is everywhere people let Him in.

You can relegate your conscience or your God to church, synagogue, or mosque, ashram, meditation center, or mountaintop. You can decide that your conscience or your God has no place in your office, your factory, or your boardroom. You can conduct your business without concern for direction or guidance, other than for the prevailing opinion of the moment.

Or, you can choose to invite your conscience or your God to be a part of your entire life, infusing every moment, every word, and every deed with the holy sparks of encounter and instruction.

When you know before whom you stand, you can feel Divine spirit—all around you and deep within you. You can know that you are standing before your God, and that your God stands with you.

When you know before whom you stand—when the "still small voice" of your conscience or your God speaks gently yet insistently to your soul—your personal life can be richer and fuller, your workplace can be open and honest, all your business dealings can be conducted with integrity, with nobility, and with truth.

When you know before whom you stand, you can join in asking the question posed by Abraham Joshua Heschel: "What is the meaning of my being?"

And with Heschel you can answer, "My quest is not for theoretical knowledge about myself....What I look for is...how to live a life that would deserve and evoke an eternal 'Amen.'"

The Business Bible's *Word to Live By*

These Ten Commandments for Creating an Ethical Workplace offer you the foundation and the formula for bringing meaning and worth, values and ethics to your job, your business, your profession.

For all their wide-ranging concerns, their profound depth and their practical relevance, these Commandments can be summed up in *one* word.

So, remember

The Business Bible's
WORD TO LIVE BY

E   *Everywhere*

T   All the *Time*

H   Be *Honest*

I   Act with *Integrity*

C   Have *Compassion*

S   For What Is *at Stake* Is
      Your Reputation,
      Your Self-esteem,
      Your Inner Peace.

And Let Us Say...

~

When you follow these Ten Commandments, you can bring meaning and worth, values and ethics, to your work and to your workplace.

You can bring honesty and trust to all your dealings, decency and dignity to all your relationships.

Not only can you do *well.*

You can do *good.*

The ability—or the desire—to make ethical choices is not something with which you are born.

Years ago an electrical blackout blanketed New York City.

To help alleviate the confusion and congestion, one young man stood at an intersection for more than six hours, directing traffic with a small flashlight.

On his way home he used the handle of his flashlight to smash a store's window and steal its contents.

The contradictory passions of selfishness and of sharing, of goodness and of greed, swirl within us all the time.

But you can *learn* to do good.

In the words of the Bible, "These commandments...not too hard for you...."

The California legislature has mandated a minimum of six hours of training in ethics each year for its members and staff.

The state of Texas has a special counsel to the governor on ethics.

Many companies are beginning to conduct seminars and hold workshops to teach ethical decision making.

When there is an awareness that there is a proactive way to make ethical decisions, that realization begins to permeate a company and affect all its dealings.

Every person who becomes sensitive to making ethical choices in the workplace becomes a teacher and model of ethics and values.

And every moment of every business day becomes a teachable moment.

Making ethical choices can be easier than it might seem.

There are only a few singularly momentous choices you will ever be called on to make.

Most of your choices can be small, everyday decisions that, taken all together, weave a pattern of behavior that guides and ultimately defines you.

Not long ago a man completed a cross-country walk.

He had started in New York, by dipping his feet into the Atlantic Ocean. He finished his journey in California, where he put his feet into the Pacific.

As he neared his destination, a large contingent from the media followed him on his final steps.

He was asked, "What was the hardest part of walking across the entire country? Was it the blazing sun? Was it the cold rains? Was it the long trek up the mountains? Was it the boredom of the flat plains? Was it the exhaustion that overcame you each night?"

The walker answered, "It was none of those things. The hardest part of walking across the whole country was the little grains of sand that kept getting into my shoes."

When you face the little things first, when you confront the small problems as they arise, you can eventually tame any monster of immorality, and slay any dragon of ethical imperfection.

And continuing in the words of the Bible, these commandments "...are not too far away from you."

Once upon a time, there was a happy, carefree little girl who lived at the edge of the forest. She loved to wander in the woods and play among the trees.

One day she lost her way.

As it grew dark and the little girl did not return home, her parents became very worried. They began calling for her and searching in the woods. But they could not find her.

Worried and afraid, they gathered their neighbors and all the people from the town to help them search for their little girl.

Meanwhile, the girl, wandering in the forest, became anxious and frightened, for it was growing darker and darker, and she could not find her way home. She tried one path and then another, but she could not find her way out of the woods.

The longer she walked, the more tired she became. Finally, she became so exhausted that when she came to a small clearing in the forest, she lay down next to a big rock and fell asleep.

Her parents and neighbors continued to search and search, but they could not find her. They called out her name over and over again, but there was no answer.

As darkness descended, many of the neighbors returned to their own homes, promising to begin the search again at the first break of dawn.

But the little girl's father would not give up. He continued his search throughout the night.

Early in the morning, just as the sun was beginning to rise, the father came to the clearing in the forest where the little girl had lain down to sleep. He saw his little girl, and ran toward her, yelling her name and making a great noise crunching the dry leaves and branches on the forest floor beneath his feet.

Awakened by the clamor and the sound of her father's voice calling out to her, the little girl looked up from her sleep and shouted out with great joy, "Daddy, Daddy, *I found you!*"

In you—in your heart and in your soul—is all the understanding, all the direction, all the commitment, that you will ever need to make ethical choices and to bring meaning to your workaday world.

In you is the possibility and the power.

In you is the vision and the promise of what you, your business—and your world—can be.

The choice to find meaning and worth in your work, the choice to bring values and ethics to your workplace, is yours.

In the words of the Bible, "…set before you are the blessing and the curse.…"

You can choose the blessing.

You can choose to do *good.*

And through the abundance of your heart and the greatness of your spirit, you can bring a full measure of blessing to everyone whose life—and work—is touched by yours.

…Amen

References

~

Biblical quotations are taken from *TANAKH, The Holy Scriptures: A New Translation According to the Traditional Hebrew Text* (Philadelphia: Jewish Publication Society, 1985), or from the author's own translation of the original Hebrew.

IN THE BEGINNING

Genesis 1:1

THE TEN COMMANDMENTS

1. "YOUR EAR SHALL HEAR; YOUR EYES SHALL SEE"

Isaiah 30:21
and Malachi 1:5

"who have eyes, but do not see."
Psalm 115:5

"if…it is no dream."
Theodor Herzl

2. "DO NOT UTTER A FALSE REPORT"

Exodus 23:1

"words that are spoken from the heart…"
Moses ibn Ezra, in *Shirat Yisrael*

3. "DO NO UNRIGHTEOUSNESS IN WEIGHTS AND MEASURES"

Leviticus 19:35

"Do not violate another's boundaries"
Deuteronomy 19:14

4. "LOVE YOUR NEIGHBOR AS YOURSELF"

Leviticus 19:18

"turn the other cheek"
after Matthew 5:39

5. "DO JUSTLY, LOVE MERCY, AND WALK HUMBLY"

Micah 6:8

"Blessed is the peacemaker"
after Matthew 5:9

"I have learned much…"
B. Talmud Ta'anit 7a

Moses drawing water from the rock
after Numbers 20

6. "BRING HEALING AND CURE"

Jeremiah 33:6

"If two men fight…"
Exodus 21:18–19

"The earth is the Lord's…"
Psalm 24:1

"If I am not for myself…"
Mishnah, Avot 1:14

"There is no wealth like health."
Mivchar HaPeninim

"Rejoice in the earth."
Psalm 97:1

7. "YOU SHALL SURELY TITHE"

Deuteronomy 14:22

"Though he needed only one portion…"
Kohelet Rabbah 7:30

"It is better to give…"
after Acts 20:35

8. "REMEMBER THE SABBATH"

Exodus 20:8

9. "ACQUIRE WISDOM"

Proverbs 4:5, 7

"Who is rich?…"
Mishnah, Avot 4:1

"Get yourself a teacher."
Mishnah, Avot 1:6

REFERENCES

"Teach me...that I may acquire a heart of wisdom"
after Psalms 90:12

10. "KNOW BEFORE WHOM YOU STAND"

popular axiom based on:
Mishnah, Avot 2:19 and
B. Talmud, Sanhedrin 22a

the "still small voice"
Job 4:16

AND LET US SAY...AMEN

"These commandments...are not too hard..." and "...are not too far away from you."
Deuteronomy 30:11

"...set before you are the blessing and the curse...."
Deuteronomy 30:19

ACKNOWLEDGMENTS

"Get yourself a Rabbi..."
Mishnah, Avot 1:6

"...my life and the length of my days"
after the prayer "Ahavat Olam"

Bibliography

~

Some of the stories (in various forms) and some of the attributed quotes in this book appear in the following works:

Aesop's Fables. New York: Grosset & Dunlap, 1947.

Alcalay, Reuven. *Words of the Wise.* Jerusalem: Masada Press, 1970.

Autry, James A. *Love and Profit: The Art of Caring Leadership.* New York: Morrow, 1991.

Bennis, Warren. *On Becoming a Leader.* Reading, Mass.: Addison-Wesley, 1989.

Buber, Martin. *Tales of the Hasidim: The Early Masters.* New York: Schocken Books, 1947.

———. *Tales of the Hasidim: The Later Masters.* New York: Schocken Books, 1948.

Certner, Simon, ed. *101 Jewish Stories for Schools, Clubs, and Camps.* New York: Jewish Education Press, 1961.

Chopra, Deepak. *Quantum Healing: Exploring the Frontiers of Mind/Body Medicine.* New York: Bantam Books, 1989.

DePree, Max. *Leadership Is an Art.* New York: Dell, 1989.

Edwards, Owen. *Upward Nobility: How to Succeed in Business Without Losing Your Soul.* New York: Crown, 1991.

Fields, Rick et al. *Chop Wood, Carry Water: A Guide to Finding Spiritual Fulfillment in Everyday Life.* Los Angeles: Tarcher, 1984.

Gibran, Kahlil. *The Prophet.* New York: Knopf, 1966.

Heschel, Abraham Joshua. *The Wisdom of Heschel,* ed. Ruth Marcus Goodhill. New York: Farrar, Straus and Giroux, 1970.

Levin, Meyer. *Classic Hassidic Tales.* New York: Citadel Press, 1966.

Miller, Ronald S. *As Above So Below.* Los Angeles: Tarcher, 1992.

Millman, Dan. *Way of the Peaceful Warrior.* Tiburon, Calif.: Kramer, 1980.

Newman, Louis I. *Hasidic Anthology.* New York: Schocken Books, 1963.

Peters, Thomas J., and Robert H. Waterman, Jr. *In Search of Excellence.* New York: Harper & Row, 1982.

Pliskin, Zelig. *Love Your Neighbor.* Brooklyn, N.Y.: Aish HaTorah, 1977.

Polsky, Howard W., and Yaella Wozner. *Everyday Miracles: The Healing Wisdom of Hasidic Stories.* Northvale, N.J.: Aronson, 1989.

Raskas, Bernard S. *Heart of Wisdom.* New York: Burning Bush Press, 1967.

———. *Heart of Wisdom, Book II.* New York: Burning Bush Press, 1979.

———. *Heart of Wisdom, Book III.* New York: United Synagogue Books, 1986.

———, ed. *Living Thoughts.* New York: Hartmore House, 1976.

Siegel, Bernie S. *Love, Medicine, and Miracles.* New York: Harper & Row, 1986.

Sinetar, Marsha. *Do What You Love, the Money Will Follow: Discovering Your Right Livelihood.* New York: Dell, 1987.

Stewart, Thomas A. "Should Your Company Save Your Soul?" *Fortune,* January 14, 1991.

Tannen, Deborah. *You Just Don't Understand.* New York: Morrow, 1990.

United Technologies Corporation, newspaper and magazine advertising.

Wolpe, David J. *The Healer of Shattered Hearts: A Jewish View of God.* New York: Holt, 1990.

~

Grateful acknowledgment is made to these authors—and the ideas in their books—who did the pioneer work in the field of meaning, values, and ethics in business, and contemporary work in the field of human development, and whose thinking influenced this work. These books are warmly recommended to those who seek in-depth discussion of specific issues addressed here in *The Business Bible*.

Blanchard, Kenneth, and Spencer Johnson. *The One-Minute Manager.* New York: Morrow, 1982.

Blanchard, Kenneth, and Norman Vincent Peale. *The Power of Ethical Management.* New York: Fawcett Crest, 1988.

Borowitz, Eugene B. *Exploring Jewish Ethics.* Detroit: Wayne State University Press, 1990.

Byham, William C. *Zapp: The Lightning of Empowerment.* New York: Harmony Books, 1988.

Chu, Chin-Ning, *Thick Face, Black Heart: Thriving, Winning, and Succeeding in Life's Every Endeavor.* Beaverton, Oreg.: AMC Publishing, 1992.

Covey, Stephen R. *Principle-Centered Leadership.* New York: Summit Books, 1990.

DePree, Max. *Leadership Jazz.* New York: Currency/Doubleday, 1992.

Drucker, Peter. *The Frontiers of Management: Where Tomorrow's Decisions Are Being Shaped Today.* New York: Perennial Library/Harper & Row, 1986.

Edelman, Marian Wright. *The Measure of Our Success: A Letter to My Children and Yours.* Boston: Beacon Press, 1992.

Ferguson, Marilyn. *The Aquarian Conspiracy: Personal and Social Transformation in the 1980s.* Los Angeles: Tarcher, 1980.

Goldzimer, Linda Silverman. *I'm First: Your Customer's Message to You.* New York: Rawson Associates, 1989.

Heider, John. *The Tao of Leadership: Leadership Strategies for a New Age.* New York: Bantam Books, 1986.

Josefowitz, Nastasha. *You're the Boss! A Guide to Managing People with Understanding and Effectiveness.* New York: Warner Books, 1985.

Kanter, Rosabeth Moss. *When Giants Learn to Dance: Mastering the Challenges of Strategy, Management, and Careers in the 1990s.* New York: Simon & Schuster, 1989.

Lewis, Hunter. *A Question of Values: Six Ways We Make the Personal Choices That Shape Our Lives.* San Francisco: Harper & Row, 1990.

Mackay, Harvey. *Beware the Naked Man Who Offers You His Shirt.* New York: Ivy Books, 1990.

———. *Swim with the Sharks Without Being Eaten Alive.* New York: Ivy Books, 1988.

Naisbitt, John, and Patricia Aburdene. *Megatrends 2000: Ten New Directions for the 1990s.* New York: Avon Books, 1990.

Ouchi, William G. *Theory Z: How American Business Can Meet the Japanese Challenge.* New York: Avon Books, 1981.

Peters, Tom, and Nancy Austin. *A Passion for Excellence: The Leadership Difference.* New York: Warner Books, 1985.

Popcorn, Faith. *The Popcorn Report.* New York: Currency/Doubleday, 1991.

Sculley, John, and John A. Byre. *Odyssey: Pepsi to Apple...The Journey of a Marketing Impresario.* New York: Perennial Library/Harper & Row, 1985.

Shames, Laurence. *The Hunger for More: Searching for Values in an Age of Greed.* New York: Times Books, 1989.

Sherwin, Byron L. *In Partnership with God: Contemporary Jewish Law and Ethics.* Syracuse, N.Y.: Syracuse University Press, 1990.

Sinetar, Marsha. *Ordinary People as Monks and Mystics: Lifestyles for Self-Discovery.* Mahwah, N.J.: Paulist Press, 1986.

Toffler, Alvin. *Powershift: Knowledge, Wealth, and Violence at the Edge of the Twenty-first Century.* New York: Bantam Books, 1990.

Walton, Sam. *Sam Walton: Made in America.* New York: Doubleday, 1992.

Watson, Thomas J., Jr. *Father, Son & Co.: My Life at IBM and Beyond.* New York: Bantam Books, 1990.

Whittemore, Hank. *CNN: The Inside Story.* Boston: Little, Brown, 1990.

Zemke, Ron. *The Service Edge: 101 Companies That Profit from Customer Care.* New York: New American Library, 1989.

Acknowledgments

~

I take great pleasure in expressing deepest thanks to those whose influence is reflected in this book:

Bruce Rotstein and the folks at Diamond Entertainment Corporation of Anaheim, California, who expressed first interest in these ideas. *Phil and Gayle Tauber,* creators of Kashi, breakfast pilaf and cereal, whose company vision reflects the best that a business can hope to be. My Rebbe, *Rabbi Jakob J. Petuchowski, Ph.D.,* of blessed memory, who continues to teach from the Great Beyond. His voice still echoes deep within me. *The Reverend James J. O'Leary, S.J.,* cherished friend, who shares with me the grandeur of the teachings of Christianity—and especially the Catholic tradition—and who creates holy ground wherever he walks. *Dr. Yehuda Shabatay,* longtime friend and wise counsel, who fulfills for me the injunction of the sages, "Get yourself a rabbi and find yourself a learning partner." *Dr. Steven Helfgot,* lifelong friend, incredibly talented educator, whose wisdom, insight, and influence permeate this book. My sisters-in-law, *Betty Kaufman* and *Norma Kaufman*—each a talented, highly successful, businesswoman—who shared with me so much of their knowledge and practical experience in the everyday world of business.

ACKNOWLEDGMENTS

Dr. Edith Eger, Theresa Pack, Victoria Bearden, Joan Bartolo, and *Roni Reynolds; Reb Zalman Schachter, Reb Shlomo Carlebach, Rabbi Moshe Shur,* and *Dr. Sheldon Kramer,* spiritual visionaries and planetary healers, who open new vistas of mind and spirit. *Sandra Dijkstra,* extraordinary literary agent, who continues to work her magic and keeps the faith. *Adrian Zackheim,* literary editor with the soul of a poet, and poet with practical wisdom, who believed in this project—and in me—who made me think and stretch and journey to places I had never been before. My parents, *Hyman and Roberta Dosick,* to whom this book is dedicated, whose ever-enduring pride and love help sustain me. My sons, *Scott and Seth.* The butterflies fly free, and I can only marvel at their brilliant colors. And, most of all, *Ellen*—wife, partner, intellectual catalyst, spiritual guide. She is "my life and the length of my days." She is my love.

Notes

Notes

Notes

Notes

Notes

Notes

Notes

Notes

About JEWISH LIGHTS Publishing

People of all faiths and backgrounds yearn for books that attract, engage, educate and spiritually inspire.

Our principal goal is to stimulate thought and help all people learn about who the Jewish People are, where they come from, and what the future can be made to hold. While people of our diverse Jewish heritage are the primary audience, our books speak to people in the Christian world as well and will broaden their understanding of Judaism and the roots of their own faith.

We bring to you authors who are at the forefront of spiritual thought and experience. While each has something different to say, they all say it in a voice that you can hear.

Our books are designed to welcome you and then to engage, stimulate and inspire. We judge our success not only by whether or not our books are beautiful and commercially successful, but by whether or not they make a difference in your life.

We at Jewish Lights take great care to produce beautiful books that present meaningful spiritual content in a form that reflects the art of making high quality books. Therefore, we want to acknowledge those who contributed to the production of this book.

Stuart M. Matlins, Publisher

PRODUCTION
Marian B. Wallace & Bridgett Taylor

EDITORIAL
Sandra Korinchak, Emily Wichland,
Martha McKinney & Amanda Dupuis

COVER DESIGN
Bridgett Taylor

COVER & TEXT PRINTING AND BINDING
Versa Press, East Peoria, Illinois

The Way Into... Series

A major 14-volume series to be completed over the next several years, *The Way Into...* provides an accessible and usable "guided tour" of the Jewish faith, its people, its history and beliefs—in total, an introduction to Judaism for adults that will enable them to understand and interact with sacred texts. Each volume is written by a major modern scholar and teacher, and is organized around an important concept of Judaism.

The Way Into... will enable all readers to achieve a real sense of Jewish cultural literacy through guided study. Forthcoming volumes include:

  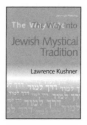 

The Way Into Torah

by *Dr. Norman J. Cohen*

What is "Torah"? What are the different approaches to studying Torah? What are the different levels of understanding Torah? For whom is the study intended? Explores the origins and development of Torah, why it should be studied and how to do it.
6 x 9, 160 pp, HC, ISBN 1-58023-028-8 **$21.95**

The Way Into Jewish Prayer

by *Dr. Lawrence A. Hoffman*

Opens the door to 3,000 years of the Jewish way to God by making available all you need to feel at home in Jewish worship. Provides basic definitions of the terms you need to know as well as thoughtful analysis of the depth that lies beneath Jewish prayer.
6 x 9, 224 pp, HC, ISBN 1-58023-027-X **$21.95**

The Way Into Jewish Mystical Tradition

by *Rabbi Lawrence Kushner*

Explains the principles of Jewish mystical thinking, their religious and spiritual significance, and how they relate to our lives. A book that allows us to experience and understand the Jewish mystical approach to our place in the world.
6 x 9, 176 pp, HC, ISBN 1-58023-029-6 **$21.95** (Avail. Nov. 2000)

The Way Into Encountering God in Judaism

by *Dr. Neil Gillman*

Explains how Jews have encountered God throughout history—and today—by exploring the many metaphors for God in Jewish tradition. Explores the Jewish tradition's passionate but also conflicting ways of relating to God as Creator, relational partner, and a force in history and nature.
6 x 9, 176 pp, HC, ISBN 1-58023-025-3 **$21.95** (Avail. Nov. 2000)

Jewish Meditation

Discovering Jewish Meditation
Instruction & Guidance for Learning an Ancient Spiritual Practice
by *Nan Fink Gefen*

Gives readers of any level of understanding the tools to learn the practice of Jewish meditation on your own, starting you on the path to a deep spiritual and personal connection to God and to greater insight about your life. 6 x 9, 208 pp, Quality PB, ISBN 1-58023-067-9 **$16.95**

Meditation from the Heart of Judaism: *Today's Teachers Share Their Practices, Techniques, and Faith*
Ed. by *Avram Davis*

A "how-to"guide for both beginning and experienced meditators, drawing on the wisdom of 22 masters of meditation who explain why and how they meditate. A detailed compendium of the experts' "best practices" offers advice and starting points. 6 x 9, 256 pp, Quality PB, ISBN 1-58023-049-0 **$16.95**; HC, ISBN 1-879045-77-X **$21.95**

The Way of Flame
A Guide to the Forgotten Mystical Tradition of Jewish Meditation
by *Avram Davis* 4½ x 8, 176 pp, Quality PB, ISBN 1-58023-060-1 **$15.95**

   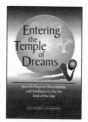 

Entering the Temple of Dreams: *Jewish Prayers, Movements, and Meditations for the End of the Day* by *Tamar Frankiel* and *Judy Greenfeld*
Nighttime spirituality is much more than bedtime prayers! Here, you'll uncover deeper meaning to familiar nighttime prayers—and learn to combine the prayers with movements and meditations to enhance your physical and psychological well-being.
7 x 10, 192 pp, Illus., Quality PB, ISBN 1-58023-079-2 **$16.95**

Minding the Temple of the Soul: *Balancing Body, Mind, and Spirit through Traditional Jewish Prayer, Movement, and Meditation*
by *Tamar Frankiel* and *Judy Greenfeld*
This new spiritual approach to physical health introduces readers to a spiritual tradition that affirms the body and enables them to reconceive their bodies in a more positive light. Focuses on traditional Jewish prayers, with exercises, movements, and meditations. 7 x 10, 184 pp, Quality PB, Illus., ISBN 1-879045-64-8 **$16.95**; Audiotape of the Blessings, Movements and Meditations (60-min. cassette), JN01 **$9.95**; Videotape of the Movements and Meditations (46-min. VHS), S507 **$20.00**

Spirituality & More

These Are the Words: *A Vocabulary of Jewish Spiritual Life*

by *Arthur Green*

What are the most essential ideas, concepts and terms that an educated person needs to know about Judaism? From *Adonai* (My Lord) to *zekhut* (merit), this enlightening and entertaining journey through Judaism teaches us the 149 core Hebrew words that constitute the basic vocabulary of Jewish spiritual life. 6 x 9, 304 pp, HC, ISBN 1-58023-024-5 **$21.95**

The Enneagram and Kabbalah: *Reading Your Soul*

by *Rabbi Howard A. Addison*

Combines two of the most powerful maps of consciousness known to humanity—The Tree of Life (the *Sefirot*) from the Jewish mystical tradition of *Kabbalah*, and the nine-pointed Enneagram—and shows how, together, they can provide a powerful tool for self-knowledge, critique, and transformation. 6 x 9, 176 pp, Quality PB, ISBN 1-58023-001-6 **$15.95**

Embracing the Covenant
Converts to Judaism Talk About Why & How

Ed. and with Intros. by *Rabbi Allan L. Berkowitz* and *Patti Moskovitz*

Through personal experiences of 20 converts to Judaism, this book illuminates reasons for converting, the quest for a satisfying spirituality, the appeal of the Jewish tradition and how conversion has changed lives—the convert's, and the lives of those close to them.
6 x 9, 192 pp, Quality PB, ISBN 1-879045-50-8 **$15.95**

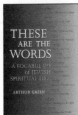    

Shared Dreams: *Martin Luther King, Jr. and the Jewish Community*
by Rabbi Marc Schneier; Preface by Martin Luther King III
6 x 9, 240 pp, HC, ISBN 1-58023-062-8 **$24.95**

Mystery Midrash: *An Anthology of Jewish Mystery & Detective Fiction*
Ed. by Lawrence W. Raphael; Preface by Joel Siegel, ABC's *Good Morning America*
6 x 9, 304 pp, Quality PB, ISBN 1-58023-055-5 **$16.95**

The Jewish Gardening Cookbook: *Growing Plants & Cooking for Holidays & Festivals*
by Michael Brown 6 x 9, 224 pp, HC, Illus., ISBN 1-58023-004-0 **$21.95**

Wandering Stars: *An Anthology of Jewish Fantasy & Science Fiction* Ed. by Jack Dann; Intro. by Isaac Asimov 6 x 9, 272 pp, Quality PB, ISBN 1-58023-005-9 **$16.95**

More Wandering Stars
An Anthology of Outstanding Stories of Jewish Fantasy and Science Fiction
Ed. by Jack Dann; Intro. by Isaac Asimov 6 x 9, 192 pp, Quality PB, ISBN 1-58023-063-6 **$16.95**

A Heart of Wisdom: *Making the Jewish Journey from Midlife through the Elder Years*
Ed. by Susan Berrin; Foreword by Harold Kushner
6 x 9, 384 pp, Quality PB, ISBN 1-58023-051-2 **$18.95**; HC, ISBN 1-879045-73-7 **$24.95**

Sacred Intentions: *Daily Inspiration to Strengthen the Spirit, Based on Jewish Wisdom*
by Rabbi Kerry M. Olitzky and Rabbi Lori Forman
4½ x 6½, 448 pp, Quality PB, ISBN 1-58023-061-X **$15.95**

Spirituality

My People's Prayer Book: *Traditional Prayers, Modern Commentaries*

Ed. by *Dr. Lawrence A. Hoffman*

This momentous, critically-acclaimed series is truly a people's prayer book, one that provides a diverse and exciting commentary to the traditional liturgy. It will help modern men and women find new wisdom and guidance in Jewish prayer, and bring liturgy into their lives. Each book includes Hebrew text, modern translation, and commentaries *from all perspectives* of the Jewish world. Vol. 1—*The Sh'ma and Its Blessings,* 7 x 10, 168 pp, HC, ISBN 1-879045-79-6 **$23.95**
Vol. 2—*The Amidah,* 7 x 10, 240 pp, HC, ISBN 1-879045-80-X **$23.95**
Vol. 3—*P'sukei D'zimrah* (Morning Psalms), 7 x 10, 240 pp, HC, ISBN 1-879045-81-8 **$23.95**
Vol. 4—*Seder K'riyat Hatorah* (Shabbat Torah Service), 7 x 10, 240 pp, ISBN 1-879045-82-6 **$23.95**
(Avail. Nov. 2000)

Voices from Genesis: *Guiding Us through the Stages of Life*

by *Dr. Norman J. Cohen*

In a brilliant blending of modern *midrash* (finding contemporary meaning from biblical texts) and the life stages of Erik Erikson's developmental psychology, the characters of Genesis come alive to give us insights for our own journeys. 6 x 9, 192 pp, HC, ISBN 1-879045-75-3 **$21.95**

  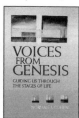 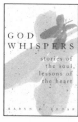 

God Whispers: *Stories of the Soul, Lessons of the Heart*
by Rabbi Karyn D. Kedar 6 x 9, 176 pp, Quality PB, ISBN 1-58023-088-1 **$15.95**;
HC, ISBN 1-58023-023-7 **$19.95**

Being God's Partner: *How to Find the Hidden Link Between Spirituality and Your Work*
by Rabbi Jeffrey K. Salkin; Intro. by Norman Lear **AWARD WINNER!**
6 x 9, 192 pp, Quality PB, ISBN 1-879045-65-6 **$16.95**; HC, ISBN 1-879045-37-0 **$19.95**

ReVisions: *Seeing Torah through a Feminist Lens* **AWARD WINNER!**
by Rabbi Elyse Goldstein 5½ x 8½, 208 pp, HC, ISBN 1-58023-047-4 **$19.95**

Soul Judaism: *Dancing with God into a New Era*
by Rabbi Wayne Dosick 5½ x 8½, 304 pp, Quality PB, ISBN 1-58023-053-9 **$16.95**

Finding Joy: *A Practical Spiritual Guide to Happiness* **AWARD WINNER!**
by Rabbi Dannel I. Schwartz with Mark Hass
6 x 9, 192 pp, Quality PB, ISBN 1-58023-009-1 **$14.95**; HC, ISBN 1-879045-53-2 **$19.95**

The Empty Chair: *Finding Hope and Joy—*
Timeless Wisdom from a Hasidic Master, Rebbe Nachman of Breslov **AWARD WINNER!**
Adapted by Moshe Mykoff and the Breslov Research Institute
4 x 6, 128 pp, Deluxe PB, 2-color text, ISBN 1-879045-67-2 **$9.95**

The Gentle Weapon: *Prayers for Everyday and Not-So-Everyday Moments*
Adapted from the Wisdom of Rebbe Nachman of Breslov by Moshe Mykoff and
S. C. Mizrahi, with the Breslov Research Institute
4 x 6, 144 pp, Deluxe PB, 2-color text, ISBN 1-58023-022-9 **$9.95**

"Who Is a Jew?" *Conversations, Not Conclusions* by Meryl Hyman
6 x 9, 272 pp, Quality PB, ISBN 1-58023-052-0 **$16.95**; HC, ISBN 1-879045-76-1 **$23.95**

Life Cycle

Jewish Paths toward Healing and Wholeness
A Personal Guide to Dealing with Suffering
by *Rabbi Kerry M. Olitzky*; Foreword by *Debbie Friedman*

"Why me?" Why do we suffer? How can we heal? Grounded in the spiritual traditions of Judaism, this book provides healing rituals, psalms and prayers that help readers initiate a dialogue with God, to guide them along the complicated path of healing and wholeness.
6 x 9, 192 pp, Quality PB, ISBN 1-58023-068-7 **$15.95**

Mourning & Mitzvah: *A Guided Journal for Walking the Mourner's Path through Grief to Healing*
by *Anne Brener*, L.C.S.W.; Foreword by *Rabbi Jack Riemer*; Intro. by *Rabbi William Cutter*

For those who mourn a death, for those who would help them, for those who face a loss of any kind, Brener teaches us the power and strength available to us in the fully experienced mourning process. 7½ x 9, 288 pp, Quality PB, ISBN 1-879045-23-0 **$19.95**

Tears of Sorrow, Seeds of Hope
A Jewish Spiritual Companion for Infertility and Pregnancy Loss
by *Rabbi Nina Beth Cardin*

A spiritual companion that enables us to mourn infertility, a lost pregnancy, or a stillbirth within the prayers, rituals, and meditations of Judaism. By drawing on the texts of tradition, it creates readings and rites of mourning, and through them provides a wellspring of compassion, solace—and hope. 6 x 9, 192 pp, HC, ISBN 1-58023-017-2 **$19.95**

Lifecycles
V. 1: *Jewish Women on Life Passages & Personal Milestones* Award Winner!
Ed. and with Intros. by Rabbi Debra Orenstein
V. 2: *Jewish Women on Biblical Themes in Contemporary Life* Award Winner!
Ed. and with Intros. by Rabbi Debra Orenstein and Rabbi Jane Rachel Litman
V. 1: 6 x 9, 480 pp, Quality PB, ISBN 1-58023-018-0 **$19.95**; HC, ISBN 1-879045-14-1 **$24.95**
V. 2: 6 x 9, 464 pp, Quality PB, ISBN 1-58023-019-9 **$19.95**; HC, ISBN 1-879045-15-X **$24.95**

Grief in Our Seasons: *A Mourner's Kaddish Companion*
by Rabbi Kerry M. Olitzky 4½ x 6½, 448 pp, Quality PB, ISBN 1-879045-55-9 **$15.95**

A Time to Mourn, A Time to Comfort: *A Guide to Jewish Bereavement and Comfort*
by Dr. Ron Wolfson 7 x 9, 336 pp, Quality PB, ISBN 1-879045-96-6 **$16.95**

When a Grandparent Dies
A Kid's Own Remembering Workbook for Dealing with Shiva and the Year Beyond
by Nechama Liss-Levinson, Ph.D.
8 x 10, 48 pp, HC, Illus., 2-color text, ISBN 1-879045-44-3 **$15.95**

So That Your Values Live On: *Ethical Wills & How to Prepare Them*
Ed. by Rabbi Jack Riemer & Professor Nathaniel Stampfer
6 x 9, 272 pp, Quality PB, ISBN 1-879045-34-6 **$17.95**

Healing/Wellness/Recovery

Jewish Pastoral Care
A Practical Handbook from Traditional and Contemporary Sources
Ed. by *Rabbi Dayle A. Friedman*

This innovative resource builds on the classic foundations of pastoral care, enriching it with uniquely Jewish traditions and wisdom. Gives today's Jewish pastoral counselors practical guidelines based in the Jewish tradition. 6 x 9, 352 pp, HC, ISBN 1-58023-078-4 **$34.95** (Avail. Nov. 2000)

Healing of Soul, Healing of Body
Spiritual Leaders Unfold the Strength & Solace in Psalms
Ed. by *Rabbi Simkha Y. Weintraub, CSW,* for The National Center for Jewish Healing

A source of solace for those who are facing illness, as well as those who care for them. Provides a wellspring of strength with inspiring introductions and commentaries by eminent spiritual leaders reflecting all Jewish movements. 6 x 9, 128 pp, Quality PB, Illus., 2-color text, ISBN 1-879045-31-1 **$14.95**

Self, Struggle & Change: *Family Conflict Stories in Genesis and Their Healing Insights for Our Lives*
by *Dr. Norman J. Cohen*

How do I find wholeness in my life and in my family's life? Here a modern master of biblical interpretation brings us greater understanding of the ancient text and of ourselves in this intriguing re-telling of conflict between husband and wife, father and son, brothers and sisters. 6 x 9, 224 pp, Quality PB, ISBN 1-879045-66-4 **$16.95**; HC, ISBN 1-879045-19-2 **$21.95**

Twelve Jewish Steps to Recovery: *A Personal Guide to Turning from Alcoholism & Other Addictions ... Drugs, Food, Gambling, Sex ...* by Rabbi Kerry M. Olitzky & Stuart A. Copans, M.D. Preface by Abraham J. Twerski, M.D.; Intro. by Rabbi Sheldon Zimmerman; "Getting Help" by JACS Foundation 6 x 9, 144 pp, Quality PB, ISBN 1-879045-09-5 **$13.95**

One Hundred Blessings Every Day: *Daily Twelve Step Recovery Affirmations, Exercises for Personal Growth & Renewal Reflecting Seasons of the Jewish Year* by Rabbi Kerry M. Olitzky, with selected meditations prepared by Rabbi James Stone Goodman, Danny Siegel, and Gordon Tucker. Foreword by Rabbi Neil Gillman, The Jewish Theological Seminary of America; Afterword by Dr. Jay Holder, Director, Exodus Treatment Center 4½ x 6½, 432 pp, Quality PB, ISBN 1-879045-30-3 **$14.95**

Recovery from Codependence: *A Jewish Twelve Steps Guide to Healing Your Soul* by Rabbi Kerry M. Olitzky; Foreword by Marc Galanter, M.D., Director, Division of Alcoholism & Drug Abuse, NYU Medical Center; Afterword by Harriet Rossetto, Director, Gateways Beit T'shuvah 6 x 9, 160 pp, Quality PB, ISBN 1-879045-32-X **$13.95**; HC, ISBN 1-879045-27-3 **$21.95**

Renewed Each Day: *Daily Twelve Step Recovery Meditations Based on the Bible* by Rabbi Kerry M. Olitzky & Aaron Z. Vol. I: *Genesis & Exodus*; Intro. by Rabbi Michael A. Signer; Afterword by JACS Foundation. Vol. II: *Leviticus, Numbers and Deuteronomy*; Intro. by Sharon M. Strassfeld; Afterword by Rabbi Harold M. Schulweis
Vol. I: 6 x 9, 224 pp, Quality PB, ISBN 1-879045-12-5 **$14.95**
Vol. II: 6 x 9, 280 pp, Quality PB, ISBN 1-879045-13-3 **$14.95**

Life Cycle & Holidays

How to Be a Perfect Stranger, In 2 Volumes
A Guide to Etiquette in Other People's Religious Ceremonies
Ed. by *Stuart M. Matlins* & *Arthur J. Magida*   AWARD WINNER!

What will happen? What do I do? What do I wear? What do I say? What should I avoid doing, wearing, saying? What are their basic beliefs? Should I bring a gift? In question-and-answer format, *How to Be a Perfect Stranger* explains the rituals and celebrations of America's major religions/denominations, helping an interested guest to feel comfortable, participate to the fullest extent possible, and avoid violating anyone's religious principles. It is not a guide to theology, nor is it presented from the perspective of any particular faith.
Vol. 1: *America's Largest Faiths*, 6 x 9, 432 pp, HC, ISBN 1-879045-39-7 **$24.95**
Vol. 2: *Other Faiths in America*, 6 x 9, 416 pp, HC, ISBN 1-879045-63-X **$24.95**

Putting God on the Guest List, 2nd Ed.
How to Reclaim the Spiritual Meaning of Your Child's Bar or Bat Mitzvah
by *Rabbi Jeffrey K. Salkin*   AWARD WINNER!

The expanded, updated, revised edition of today's most influential book (over 60,000 copies in print) about finding core spiritual values in American Jewry's most misunderstood ceremony.
6 x 9, 224 pp, Quality PB, ISBN 1-879045-59-1 **$16.95**; HC, ISBN 1-879045-58-3 **$24.95**

For Kids—Putting God on Your Guest List
How to Claim the Spiritual Meaning of Your Bar or Bat Mitzvah
by Rabbi Jeffrey K. Salkin   6 x 9, 144 pp, Quality PB, ISBN 1-58023-015-6 **$14.95**

Bar/Bat Mitzvah Basics
A Practical Family Guide to Coming of Age Together
Ed. by Cantor Helen Leneman   6 x 9, 240 pp, Quality PB, ISBN 1-879045-54-0 **$16.95**;
HC, ISBN 1-879045-51-6 **$24.95**

The New Jewish Baby Book   AWARD WINNER!
Names, Ceremonies, & Customs—A Guide for Today's Families
by Anita Diamant   6 x 9, 336 pp, Quality PB, ISBN 1-879045-28-1 **$16.95**

Hanukkah: The Art of Jewish Living
by Dr. Ron Wolfson   7 x 9, 192 pp, Quality PB, Illus., ISBN 1-879045-97-4 **$16.95**

The Shabbat Seder: The Art of Jewish Living
by Dr. Ron Wolfson   7 x 9, 272 pp, Quality PB, Illus., ISBN 1-879045-90-7 **$16.95**
Also available are these helpful companions to *The Shabbat Seder*: Booklet of the Blessings and Songs, ISBN 1-879045-91-5 **$5.00**; Audiocassette of the Blessings, DN03 **$6.00**; Teacher's Guide, ISBN 1-879045-92-3 **$4.95**

The Passover Seder: The Art of Jewish Living
by Dr. Ron Wolfson   7 x 9, 352 pp, Quality PB, Illus., ISBN 1-879045-93-1 **$16.95**
Also available are these helpful companions to *The Passover Seder*: Passover Workbook, ISBN 1-879045-94-X **$6.95**; Audiocassette of the Blessings, DN04 **$6.00**; Teacher's Guide, ISBN 1-879045-95-8 **$4.95**

Theology/Philosophy

Torah of the Earth: *Exploring 4,000 Years of Ecology in Jewish Thought*
In 2 Volumes Ed. by *Rabbi Arthur Waskow*

Major new resource offering us an invaluable key to understanding the intersection of ecology and Judaism. Leading scholars provide us with a guided tour of ecological thought from four major Jewish viewpoints. Vol. 1: *Biblical Israel & Rabbinic Judaism,* 6 x 9, 272 pp, Quality PB, ISBN 1-58023-086-5 **$19.95**; Vol. 2: *Zionism & Eco-Judaism,* 6 x 9, 336 pp, Quality PB, ISBN 1-58023-087-3 **$19.95**

Broken Tablets: *Restoring the Ten Commandments and Ourselves*
Ed. by *Rabbi Rachel S. Mikva*; Intro. by *Rabbi Lawrence Kushner*; Afterword by *Rabbi Arnold Jacob Wolf* **AWARD WINNER!**

Twelve outstanding spiritual leaders each share profound and personal thoughts about these biblical commands and why they have such a special hold on us.
6 x 9, 192 pp, HC, ISBN 1-58023-066-0 **$21.95**

Evolving Halakhah: *A Progressive Approach to Traditional Jewish Law*
by *Rabbi Dr. Moshe Zemer*

Innovative and provocative, this book affirms the system of traditional Jewish law, *halakhah,* as flexible enough to accommodate the changing realities of each generation. It shows that the traditional framework for understanding the Torah's commandments can be the living heart of Jewish life for all Jews. 6 x 9, 480 pp, HC, ISBN 1-58023-002-4 **$40.00**

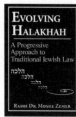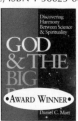

God & the Big Bang
Discovering Harmony Between Science & Spirituality **AWARD WINNER!**
by Daniel C. Matt
6 x 9, 216 pp, Quality PB, ISBN 1-879045-89-3 **$16.95**; HC, ISBN 1-879045-48-6 **$21.95**

Israel—A Spiritual Travel Guide **AWARD WINNER!**
A Companion for the Modern Jewish Pilgrim
by Rabbi Lawrence A. Hoffman 4¼ x 10, 256 pp, Quality PB, ISBN 1-879045-56-7 **$18.95**

Godwrestling—Round 2: *Ancient Wisdom, Future Paths* **AWARD WINNER!**
by Rabbi Arthur Waskow
6 x 9, 352 pp, Quality PB, ISBN 1-879045-72-9 **$18.95**; HC, ISBN 1-879045-45-1 **$23.95**

Ecology & the Jewish Spirit: *Where Nature & the Sacred Meet* Ed. and with Intros. by Ellen Bernstein 6 x 9, 288 pp, Quality PB, ISBN 1-58023-082-2 **$16.95**;
HC, ISBN 1-879045-88-5 **$23.95**

Israel: *An Echo of Eternity* by Abraham Joshua Heschel; New Intro. by
Dr. Susannah Heschel 5½ x 8, 272 pp, Quality PB, ISBN 1-879045-70-2 **$18.95**

The Earth Is the Lord's: *The Inner World of the Jew in Eastern Europe*
by Abraham Joshua Heschel 5½ x 8, 112 pp, Quality PB, ISBN 1-879045-42-7 **$13.95**

A Passion for Truth: *Despair and Hope in Hasidism* by Abraham Joshua Heschel
5½ x 8, 352 pp, Quality PB, ISBN 1-879045-41-9 **$18.95**

Theology/Philosophy

A Heart of Many Rooms
Celebrating the Many Voices within Judaism
by *Dr. David Hartman* AWARD WINNER!

Named a *Publishers Weekly* "Best Book of the Year." Addresses the spiritual and theological questions that face all Jews and all people today. From the perspective of traditional Judaism, Hartman shows that commitment to both Jewish tradition and to pluralism can create understanding between people of different religious convictions.
6 x 9, 352 pp, HC, ISBN 1-58023-048-2 **$24.95**

A Living Covenant: *The Innovative Spirit in Traditional Judaism*
by *Dr. David Hartman* AWARD WINNER!

Winner, National Jewish Book Award. Hartman reveals a Judaism grounded in covenant—a relational framework—informed by the metaphor of marital love rather than that of parent-child dependency. 6 x 9, 368 pp, Quality PB, ISBN 1-58023-011-3 **$18.95**

The Death of Death: *Resurrection and Immortality in Jewish Thought*
by *Dr. Neil Gillman* AWARD WINNER!

Does death end life, or is it the passage from one stage of life to another? This National Jewish Book Award Finalist explores the original and compelling argument that Judaism, a religion often thought to pay little attention to the afterlife, not only offers us rich ideas on the subject—but delivers a deathblow to death itself. 6 x 9, 336 pp, Quality PB, ISBN 1-58023-081-4 **$18.95**; HC, ISBN 1-879045-61-3 **$23.95**

 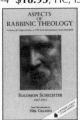   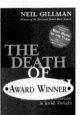

Aspects of Rabbinic Theology by Solomon Schechter; New Intro. by Dr. Neil Gillman
6 x 9, 448 pp, Quality PB, ISBN 1-879045-24-9 **$19.95**

The Last Trial: *On the Legends and Lore of the Command to Abraham to Offer Isaac as a Sacrifice* by Shalom Spiegel; New Intro. by Judah Goldin
6 x 9, 208 pp, Quality PB, ISBN 1-879045-29-X **$17.95**

Judaism and Modern Man: *An Interpretation of Jewish Religion* by Will Herberg; New Intro. by Dr. Neil Gillman 5½ x 8½, 336 pp, Quality PB, ISBN 1-879045-87-7 **$18.95**

Seeking the Path to Life AWARD WINNER!
Theological Meditations on God and the Nature of People, Love, Life and Death
by Rabbi Ira F. Stone
6 x 9, 160 pp, Quality PB, ISBN 1-879045-47-8 **$14.95**; HC, ISBN 1-879045-17-6 **$19.95**

The Spirit of Renewal: *Finding Faith after the Holocaust* AWARD WINNER!
by Rabbi Edward Feld
6 x 9, 224 pp, Quality PB, ISBN 1-879045-40-0 **$16.95**

Tormented Master: *The Life and Spiritual Quest of Rabbi Nahman of Bratslav*
by Dr. Arthur Green
6 x 9, 416 pp, Quality PB, ISBN 1-879045-11-7 **$18.95**

Your Word Is Fire: *The Hasidic Masters on Contemplative Prayer*
Ed. and Trans. with a New Introduction by Dr. Arthur Green and Dr. Barry W. Holtz
6 x 9, 160 pp, Quality PB, ISBN 1-879045-25-7 **$14.95**

Children's Spirituality

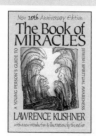

Children's Spirituality

God Said Amen

by *Sandy Eisenberg Sasso*
Full-color illus. by *Avi Katz*

For ages 4 & up

MULTICULTURAL, NONDENOMINATIONAL, NONSECTARIAN

A warm and inspiring tale of two kingdoms: Midnight Kingdom is overflowing with water but has no oil to light its lamps; Desert Kingdom is blessed with oil but has no water to grow its gardens. The kingdoms' rulers ask God for help but are too stubborn to ask each other. It takes a minstrel, a pair of royal riding-birds and their young keepers, and a simple act of kindness to show that they need only reach out to each other to find God's answer to their prayers.

9 x 12, 32 pp, HC, Full-color illus., ISBN 1-58023-080-6 **$16.95**

For Heaven's Sake

by *Sandy Eisenberg Sasso*; Full-color illus. by *Kathryn Kunz Finney*
MULTICULTURAL, NONDENOMINATIONAL, NONSECTARIAN

For ages 4 & up

Everyone talked about heaven: "Thank heavens." "Heaven forbid." "For heaven's sake, Isaiah." But no one would say what heaven was or how to find it. So Isaiah decides to find out, by seeking answers from many different people. "This book is a reminder of how well Sandy Sasso knows the minds of children. But it may surprise—and delight—readers to find how well she knows us grown-ups too." —*Maria Harris*, National Consultant in Religious Education, and author of *Teaching and Religious Imagination* 9 x 12, 32 pp, HC, Full-color illus., ISBN 1-58023-054-7 **$16.95**

But God Remembered: Stories of Women from Creation to the Promised Land

by *Sandy Eisenberg Sasso*; Full-color illus. by *Bethanne Andersen*
NONDENOMINATIONAL, NONSECTARIAN

For ages 8 & up

A fascinating collection of four different stories of women only briefly mentioned in biblical tradition and religious texts. Award-winning author Sasso vibrantly brings to life courageous and strong women from ancient tradition; all teach important values through their actions and faith. "Exquisite. . . . A book of beauty, strength and spirituality." —*Association of Bible Teachers* 9 x 12, 32 pp, HC, Full-color illus., ISBN 1-879045-43-5 **$16.95**

God in Between

by *Sandy Eisenberg Sasso*; Full-color illus. by *Sally Sweetland*
MULTICULTURAL, NONDENOMINATIONAL, NONSECTARIAN

For ages 4 & up

If you wanted to find God, where would you look? A magical, mythical tale that teaches that God can be found where we are: within all of us and the relationships between us. "This happy and wondrous book takes our children on a sweet and holy journey into God's presence." —*Rabbi Wayne Dosick, Ph.D.*, author of *Golden Rules* and *Soul Judaism*
9 x 12, 32 pp, HC, Full-color illus., ISBN 1-879045-86-9 **$16.95**

Children's Spirituality

In Our Image
God's First Creatures
by *Nancy Sohn Swartz*
Full-color illus. by *Melanie Hall*

For ages 4 & up

NONDENOMINATIONAL, NONSECTARIAN

A playful new twist on the Creation story—from the perspective of the animals. Celebrates the interconnectedness of nature and the harmony of all living things. "The vibrantly colored illustrations nearly leap off the page in this delightful interpretation." —*School Library Journal*

"A message all children should hear, presented in words and pictures that children will find irresistible." —*Rabbi Harold Kushner*, author of *When Bad Things Happen to Good People*

9 x 12, 32 pp, HC, Full-color illus., ISBN 1-879045-99-0 **$16.95**

God's Paintbrush

For ages 4 & up

by *Sandy Eisenberg Sasso*; Full-color illus. by *Annette Compton*
MULTICULTURAL, NONDENOMINATIONAL, NONSECTARIAN

Invites children of all faiths and backgrounds to encounter God openly in their own lives. Wonderfully interactive; provides questions adult and child can explore together at the end of each episode. "An excellent way to honor the imaginative breadth and depth of the spiritual life of the young." —*Dr. Robert Coles*, Harvard University
11 x 8½, 32 pp, HC, Full-color illus., ISBN 1-879045-22-2 **$16.95**

Also available: A Teacher's Guide: **A Guide for Jewish & Christian Educators and Parents**
8½ x 11, 32 pp, PB, ISBN 1-879045-57-5 **$6.95**

God's Paintbrush Celebration Kit 9½ x 12, HC, Includes 5 sessions/40 full-color Activity Sheets and Teacher Folder with complete instructions, ISBN 1-58023-050-4 **$21.95**

In God's Name

For ages 4 & up

by *Sandy Eisenberg Sasso*; Full-color illus. by *Phoebe Stone*
MULTICULTURAL, NONDENOMINATIONAL, NONSECTARIAN

Like an ancient myth in its poetic text and vibrant illustrations, this award-winning modern fable about the search for God's name celebrates the diversity and, at the same time, the unity of all the people of the world. "What a lovely, healing book!" —*Madeleine L'Engle*
9 x 12, 32 pp, HC, Full-color illus., ISBN 1-879045-26-5 **$16.95**

What Is God's Name? (A Board Book)

For ages 0–4

An abridged board book version of the award-winning *In God's Name.*
5 x 5, 24 pp, Board, Full-color illus., ISBN 1-893361-10-1 **$7.95**

Spirituality—The Kushner Series

Honey from the Rock, Special Anniversary Edition
An Introduction to Jewish Mysticism
by *Lawrence Kushner*

An insightful and absorbing introduction to the ten gates of Jewish mysticism and how it applies to daily life. "The easiest introduction to Jewish mysticism you can read."
6 x 9, 176 pp, Quality PB, ISBN 1-58023-073-3 **$15.95**

Eyes Remade for Wonder
The Way of Jewish Mysticism and Sacred Living
A Lawrence Kushner Reader

Intro. by *Thomas Moore*

Whether you are new to Kushner or a devoted fan, you'll find inspiration here. With samplings from each of Kushner's works, and a generous amount of new material, this book is to be read and reread, each time discovering deeper layers of meaning in our lives.
6 x 9, 240 pp, Quality PB, ISBN 1-58023-042-3 **$16.95**; HC, ISBN 1-58023-014-8 **$23.95**

Invisible Lines of Connection
Sacred Stories of the Ordinary
by *Lawrence Kushner* **AWARD WINNER!**

Through his everyday encounters with family, friends, colleagues and strangers, Kushner takes us deeply into our lives, finding flashes of spiritual insight in the process.
6 x 9, 160 pp, Quality PB, ISBN 1-879045-98-2 **$15.95**; HC, ISBN 1-879045-52-4 **$21.95**

The Book of Letters
A Mystical Hebrew Alphabet **AWARD WINNER!**
by Lawrence Kushner
Popular HC Edition, 6 x 9, 80 pp, 2-color text, ISBN 1-879045-00-1 **$24.95**; *Deluxe Gift Edition*, 9 x 12, 80 pp, HC, 2-color text, ornamentation, slipcase, ISBN 1-879045-01-X **$79.95**; *Collector's Limited Edition*, 9 x 12, 80 pp, HC, gold-embossed pages, hand-assembled slipcase. With silkscreened print. Limited to 500 signed and numbered copies, ISBN 1-879045-04-4 **$349.00**

The Book of Words
Talking Spiritual Life, Living Spiritual Talk **AWARD WINNER!**
by Lawrence Kushner 6 x 9, 160 pp, Quality PB, 2-color text, ISBN 1-58023-020-2 **$16.95**; 152 pp, HC, ISBN 1-879045-35-4 **$21.95**

God Was in This Place & I, i Did Not Know
Finding Self, Spirituality & Ultimate Meaning
by Lawrence Kushner 6 x 9, 192 pp, Quality PB, ISBN 1-879045-33-8 **$16.95**

The River of Light: *Jewish Mystical Awareness*
by Lawrence Kushner 6 x 9, 192 pp, Quality PB, ISBN 1-879045-03-6 **$14.95**

   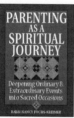